Life Stories of a Hero

Selections from the poetry of
Howard Palmer, native Oregonian,
1907-1988

by

BC McGregor

iUniverse, Inc.
New York   Bloomington

Life Stories of a Hero

Selections from the poetry of Howard Palmer, native Oregonian, 1907-1988

iUniverse books may be ordered through booksellers or by contacting:

iUniverse
1663 Liberty Drive
Bloomington, IN 47403
www.iuniverse.com
1-800-Authors (1-800-288-4677)

ISBN: 978-1-4401-2216-3 (sc)
ISBN: 978-1-4401-2217-0 (ebook)

Printed in the United States of America

iUniverse rev. date: 4/20/2009

Howard Palmer, my Grandpa, my hero.

An 'awe inspiring' man who overcame some rough trials (please read "How I learned the Logging Trade" and "Country Boy's Lament"), and then gave us "Children" and "My Prayer For Today".

His education was life experience, and Life magazine, and through his wisdom he taught us all, "Life is to be enjoyed and respected." Add to that his snappy wit and engaging humor, most certainly, there are pieces that will make you go, "hmmmm".

So with undying respect for everything he did, I am very proud to present an enjoyable legacy of Howard Palmer.

Respectfully,
Bonnie Claire 'BC' McGregor

Howard Palmer was born October 11, 1908, and was the quintessential native Oregonian from the small coastal town of Waldport, Oregon.

He lived a hard life, but turned out to be a hero to his family, friends, children, and of course, me.

This very special man was my grandpa, and that made me one very lucky little girl.

His life story is told through poetry and humor; and I am honored to present, *"Life Stories of a Hero"*.

Bonnie Claire 'BC' McGregor

Table of Contents

Chapter One: A Wise Man Once Said

Chapter Two: Two Passions ... History and Nature

Chapter Three: *The Near and Dear*

Chapter Four: *A Different Side*

CHAPTER ONE:

A Wise Man Once Said

MY PRAYER FOR TODAY

O, give me grace, Dear Lord, I pray,
To face the trials of each new day.

Yes, give me, Lord, the love I need,
To overcome my selfish greed.

And if, Oh Lord, my way is steep,
Give me strength, my faith to keep.

Forgive me, Lord, for things I say,
And evil done along the way.

Help me to go that second mile,
And aid my brother with a smile.

The strength I need, Oh Lord, supply,
When temptations lure, I would deny.

For when my allotted days are o're,
Please guide me to the Golden Shore.

And when I lie beneath the sod,
Write on my stone, "He worshiped God."

March, 1975

GOD'S HANDIWORK

"No man may live", the Bible says,
"If he has seen God's face."
Yet, I have seen His handiwork,
In almost every place.

His voice speaks through the thunder,
When the lightning stalks about.
I am sure that he's in Heaven,
When the evening stars come out.

How may we find more beauty,
Than in autumn's falling leaves?
Or in a summer sunset,
He so masterfully weaves.

You may find Him too, my friend,
If you but hesitate,
And in that head-long dash through life,
Just pause and meditate!

You will find that all your worry,
Isn't worth the time it took.
And that God is always waiting,
If you'll take the time to look.

I'm sure, on earth, that you and I,
Will never see God's face.
But should we look, His handiwork,
Is about us, every place!

July 1976

IT'S EASTER TIME

When winter time is far behind,
And spring in all it's glory,
Promises a summer sun to shine,
Foretold by prophet's story.

It's Easter time! A cherry tree,
In my yard stands a' blooming.
Arrayed in pink and matching green,
A symphony of grooming.

Though lowly man can only stand,
Transfixed with awe and wonder,
At beauty so beyond his scope,
Inept by his own blunder.

An Easter lily! Green and white,
Proclaims that Christ has risen.
That man may kneel before his God,
And find his sins forgiven.

With renewed faith, a world we face,
Beset with mass confusion,
Sorely tried on every side,
By Satan's false elusions.

But still we seek, to help the weak,
Or raise a fallen brother.
We put our shoulder to the wheel,
And encourage one another.

To fight the fight, to run the race,
And know you've done your best.
Accept all men for what they are,
In this, you shall be blessed.

July 1974

WHAT THEN, MY FRIEND, IS THE ANSWER?

Are the days of our life span numbered?
Does the "Grim Reaper" ride on our trail?
Do you feel his hot breath on the back of your neck?
If so, it will be of no avail.

What then, my friend, is the answer?
As the sand from the glass quickly flows.
Will we find our fortune is waiting,
Or be dashed into dust by our foes?

Too long we have lived in a world of our own.
A fragile maze of our making.
Contributing nothing to add to the whole.
Noted only for greed and for taking.

We watch in dismay, as our days speed away.
Some lives leave no prints in the sand.
As we shake with fear, the "Four Horsemen" appear,
To ride roughshod over the land.

Surely, there must be an answer.
Life here cannot be the end.
For man, created in God's image,
Will not be cast out in the end.

With faith, we must wait for the answer.
This spark we call life, will endure.
Burning brightly, we'll face, in some other place,
The judgment of God, I am sure.

So, live your life as God must have intended.
Be kind to the people you meet.
Have love in your heart, right from the start,
And a smile for each one that you greet.

Continued...

Fear not, for what comes tomorrow,
For tomorrow will fend for itself.
Your deeds will be noted in God's record book,
Where it lays on God's library shelf.

March 1975

A WHISTLE IN THE NIGHT

At night, I lie and listen,
To a freight train's lonesome wail,
As it charges through the darkness,
Over endless miles of rails.

I visualize the headlamp,
As it scans the unknown dark.
It bares the souls of power poles,
Standing stiff and straight and stark.

Then I wonder where it's going.
And what its load might be.
Could it be gold, from the Yukon?
Or maybe coal from Tennessee?

Perhaps it's wheat from Russia,
Or from Montana's golden store?
Might it be teak wood from Calcutta,
Or tea from China's shore?

Could it be diamonds for a wedding?
Silk and satin for a bride?
A tuxedo for a bridegroom,
With a black strip down the side?

As the train goes on to nowhere,
I am lost in Morpheus arms.
Lulled at last, to peaceful slumber,
By the freight train's many charms.

September 1975

THE MYSTERY OF A NEW DAY

Have you seen the colors,
That accompany the dawn?
Have you seen the darkness waning?
As another day is born?

Have you seen the sun awaken,
From his sleep behind the hill?
Then appear, to start his vigil,
And obey the Master's will.

Mere man can only marvel,
At the ever changing light,
As each succeeding moment,
Brings new vistas into sight.

Then, should you listen quietly,
To the encircling sound,
Played by the birds to greet the dawn,
A symphony profound!

The moon and stars, their stations keep,
But with the coming dawn,
Their cheery light, that lit the night,
In moments will be gone.

Oh! Maker of the universe,
In awe, we stand dumb-founded!
By the greatness of the mysteries,
By which we are surrounded.

March 1975

STRIVE TO BE THE BEST

You ask me, my son, for a guideline.
A target to aim for, a star!
To which you might hitch your wagon.
A Mecca you watch from afar.

It's so easy to follow the leader,
But with drive, you could be the lead!
You'll find it takes guts to fight for what's right,
Where ever there's oppression and greed.

First and foremost, above all else,
To yourself, you must always be true.
And honesty, you'll find is the best policy,
No matter, what ever you do!

Whatever you strive for, be a leader.
Be the one who stands out in a crowd.
Be the one who is known as a listener.
Not the one that is known 'cause he's loud.

Be thoughtful and kind to your family.
Remember, they are counting on you,
To provide them with love and a living.
It's the least thing a father can do!

It's no shame to be known as a Christian,
With love in your heart for all men.
And if you want good will from your peers,
You must first, be a friend to them.

December 1974

I MARVEL AT THE MANY THINGS

I marvel at the many things,
That I see, each day.
I wonder about the mysteries,
I find along life's way.

I have a home and happiness.
I have a host of friends.
Why do I, a sinful man,
Merit all the blessings sent?

My mind becomes all jumbled,
When I try to figure out,
Why I've been blessed above the rest,
To me, there is no doubt.

When I see those all around me,
Down-trodden and in pain,
Then I see the rich surrounded,
By all their ill-gotten gain.

I watch them in the market place,
As manfully they strive.
Each one acquiring ulcers,
Compensation for their drive.

They peer around the corners,
As if someone's on their trail.
Their lives revert to misery,
Fearful they might fail.

It's then, I'm very grateful,
For the quiet life I've spent,
As I note the rich man's worries,
My station leaves me quite content!

November 1978

WHERE ARE MY SONS?

When my sons were young and they played about,
Running in and running out.
I would ask at dinner time,
"Where are my sons?"

Then came school and study time.
Or playing with other kids in the bright sunshine.
And when I found that I had need of one,
I would ask my wife, "Where are my sons?"

In nineteen-eighteen, we saw them go,
To fight in the mud, and die in the snow.
When it was done, how many fathers asked?
"Where are my sons?

Again in the fifties, they had to go,
To Pork Chop Hill and Ganwon-do.
American fighters, every one,
And a father asks, "Where are my sons?

In the sixties, Uncle Sam sent men to Vietnam.
Sixty thousand spirits returned to God!
While we, in grief ask, "Is it done?"
And a father sobs, "Where is my son?"

Then, one day, my sons were gone!
One in Okinawa, one in Saigon. And I cried.
But they came home; I was a lucky one,
Who never had to ask, "Where are my sons?"

And I am grateful....

Date Unknown

CAN MAN DESTROY THIS WORLD?

Life just seems to be full of hang-ups,
As we go along day to day.
And the things that we valued most highly,
One by one, are slipping away.

Let's go back to the time when our "brother",
Was anyone needing a hand.
Or a neighbor might be a small baby,
In some distant far off land.

Let's return to the use of the "Golden Rule".
Let us stamp out hatred and greed!
Then, selfishness would be a thing of the past,
And man, from his lusts, will be freed!

The gay life of Sodom and Gomorrah,
Are the pathways that lead us to Hell!
The idols we worship, have fallen,
And lay molding, in dust, where they fell!

We are now at the door of decision!
To choose the wrong way, we dare not.
We throw our hands up in horror,
As we watch our kids go to "pot"!

This world was not made in a moment!
It took the good Lord seven days.
But we are doing our best to destroy it,
And we will search until we find the ways!

April 1971

TIME SURE DO FLY, DON'T IT?

I cant' help but think
Of the days of my youth,
As I face all the facts
That I know are the truth.
And I wonder just what
The future will do.
Time sure do fly, don't it?

I wait for the sun
To rise every day.
In my hair I see,
A little more gray.
And I find it hard to hear
All that you say.
Time. It sure do fly, don't it?

I watch the small children
As they run and play.
Their energy seems to last
all through the day.
Why, I can recall how I
Played the same way.
Time sure do fly, don't it?

I sit on the bench
With my hands on my cane.
The aches in my joints
Is a'causing me pain.
In fact, my arthritis
Will drive me insane.
Time. It sure do fly, don't it?

Continued...

12

It seems nowadays, I don't
Breath quite so well.
After I walk,
I must rest a spell.
And when they ask me, "Who's coming?"
I can hardly tell.
Time sure do fly, don't it?

It seems that my eye sight
Is getting much dimmer.
And on my head,
My hair seems much thinner.
I even take pills
Before I eat dinner.
Time. It sure do fly, don't it?

Seems they're building the stairs a lot steeper.
Each winter the snowfall
Seems a lot deeper.
And I can remember when things
Were a whole lot cheaper.
Time sure do fly, don't it?

Now when I awake,
I see on the chest,
My teeth in a glass,
Where I put them to rest.
I'm mighty thankful that toothache
Will never be a pest.
Time. It sure do fly, don't it?

The kids of today
Are sure growing tall.
The newsprint I read
Seems exceptionally small
And before I know it,
Summer's changed into fall.
Time sure do fly, don't it?

March 1971

OUR LIFE

Our life is like a railroad train,
Streaming down the track.
We have a one-way ticket,
Cause we won't be coming back.

Can't tell you what there is to see,
Or what it all will mean.
For no one yet, has ever returned,
To tell what they have seen.

Sometimes there'll be no sunshine
As the days grow dark and drear,
Where the heart is filled with anguish,
And the soul is filled with fear.

But life is for the living,
And death is not the end.
For success, it will be measured
By the number of your friends.

You'll be judged by what's inside you,
And how you passed the test.
Not by the size of bank accounts,
Or real estate possessed.

Don't ask me how that ride will end.
It all depends on you,
The people that you ride with,
And what you say or do.

As the train roars forever onward,
To its tryst with destiny.
We can only sit and watch it vanish,
As it heads for Eternity.

Date unknown

NO WAY BUT UP

Which way but up, can a man go,
When he's knocked off his feet?
What makes him strive to rise again,
While lying in the street?

What makes him aim for higher plains,
When everything looks bleak?
When fate denies each effort,
For the fortune he would seek?

But yet, he struggles onward,
Refusing to give in.
Fighting back with vigor,
When he takes one on the chin.

The sands of time will witness,
The pathways that he'll trod,
Seeking his ideals,
Or worshiping his God.

We know all will turn out better,
Because we fought and found,
There is no way but up to go,
When fate has knocked us down.

December 1971

THE SIGNS OF THE TIMES

Christmas has come,
And Christmas has gone.
Just as it has,
Since Bethlehem's dawn.

We watch as the crowds hurry,
From place to place.
They seem to run faster,
And pick up the pace.

Rushing madly about,
Searching for things,
Notions and lotions,
And toys and rings.

All kinds of gadgets,
That people don't need.
All kinds of books.
That people won't read.

Our world is filled
With mistrust and ill will.
Why then, give boys toys,
That will teach them to kill?

The news that we watch,
And hear every day,
Leaves much to desire,
And very little to say.

The people in Congress,
The cons and the pros,
Have promised us these,
And promised us those.

Continued...

While the people's disgust,
Continually grows,
The stink that arises,
Leaves us holding our nose!

Inflation is with us.
Prices all rise.
We look at our taxes,
With tears in our eyes.

The Social Security fund,
Is about to go broke.
Getting by on what's left,
Is a practical joke!

For ages, the old folk,
Have prophesied doom.
They know that we'll starve,
And they glory in gloom.

They feel sure that all humans,
Are headed for Hell!
And everything's been that way,
For quite a long spell.

So before I give up,
And am laid 'neath the sod,
I would like to speak out,
For the goodness of God.

For we have our faith in God,
On which to rely,
And our hope to sustain us,
In the sweet "bye and bye".

December 1977

THIS THING CALLED TIME

What is this thing called time?
When did it start to flow?
Where did it get its beginning?
And where will it finally go?

What is it composed of?
Why is it so exact?
Why is it hard to see ahead,
Yet so easy to look back?

Why must its source be hidden,
From those who would like to know?
Just what, is this thing called time,
And the force that makes it go!

Where did time have its beginning?
Who started it to flow?
My mind grows numb when no answers come,
Because, no one seems to know!

I'll give up, I guess, with the questions.
My mind spins till I hardly can see!
I'll leave the answers, for others to find,
And accept what "will be, will be?"

April 1975

POLLUTION

We are told that pollution will kill us!
Now, I'm sure as can be that it will.
We will know it's too late, when we all suffocate.
In fact, we'll be over the hill.

Too long, we have watched the pure water,
Disappear with a "slurp" down the drain.
We can't seem to use it, unless we abuse it.
And it will never pass this way again!

The pure air, that we once took for granted,
Is no longer as clean as we think.
The wise men who know, say, "We'd better go slow,
Or we'll soon be a race that's extinct."

There were once great streams full of fishes.
Today, no fish can be found!
Where our tent used to sit, there's a garbage pit,
That is surely polluting the ground.

Today! Is the day for the answers.
No longer do we dare hesitate!
So, unless we reverse, it shall only get worse.
I fear we have sealed our own fate!

March 1977

A RICH MAN

Have you ever stopped to wonder?
Why man toils in discontent?
Why his energy's exhausted,
And his time is so misspent?

He's had his share of trouble,
Feels down-trodden by the strife.
Hard luck seems to dog him,
But he seeks a better life.

Don't listen to the voices, friend,
That proclaim the day of doom,
You're only hidden by a cloud,
And not the final gloom.

Why, you have things no one can steal,
And none can tell their worth.
Why feel tired, and bent, and beaten?
Brace up, my friend, you've got the earth.

Why, the blue sky's for the grabbing,
With the heavens shining through,
And the flowers that grace the valley,
Were all put there just for you.

Don't worry that you're dressed in tatters.
Overhead you have the sky!
Above, the many blessings,
You've a soul that will not die!

So never mind your station, brother,
Though it seems headed for a fall.
When God's love dwells within you,
You are rich beyond recall!

Date Unknown

THAT'S WHAT IT'S ALL ABOUT

As I arise each morning,
To greet a brand new day,
I pray the Lord will guide me
As I struggle down the way.

That He'll fill my heart, so full of love,
For all of those I meet.
That I may feed a hungry child,
Or wash a beggar's feet.

Lord, put compassion in my soul,
And never let me doubt,
That friendship makes the world go round.
That's what it's all about.

Why, I could be a millionaire,
And still not have a friend,
Who would help me when I needed help,
Or stay with me to the end?

Should I acquire the universe,
While within me no love dwells,
As I gloat over ill-gotten gains,
And my pathway leads toward Hell.

I am aware that God doth dwell,
On earth and in Heaven above,
And that which makes the world go 'round,
Is love, love, love.

AND THAT IS WHAT IT'S ALL ABOUT!!!!

December 1974

A COUNTRY BOY'S LAMENT

I'm a country boy, lost in the city.
I came seeking fortune and fame.
But now I am beaten, I'm bent, and I'm broke,
Without a cent to my name.

I am cast with the weak and the wanton.
The prostitutes, pimps and the punks.
I have slept on the floor, with a fifty cent whore,
And I've walked the streets pushing "junk".

Oh Lord, how I've hated each moment.
How I've longed for fresh air and the sun.
A fresh wind blowing in from the sea,
And rest, when a day's work is done.

How often I have wanted to chuck it,
To return to the quiet and peace,
To throw off the chains that bind me,
But Fate won't relent or release.

I cringe at the sound of the city.
I quiver, and shiver, and cry,
When the fire engines scream out their warning,
As down the street, they pass by.

Continued...

I watch as the poor beaten wage slave,
Defeated, bedraggled, betrayed,
Hurrying and scurrying like ants from a hill,
Seeking freedom to follow his trade.

When I hear all the noise of the city,
I dream of the Oregon coast,
And enjoying a stream that's running clear and clean,
Is the one thing that I long for the most.

There is hatred and greed in the city!
There is danger and doom everywhere.
I know I must go to that fog-covered glen,
And again fill my lungs with clean air.

How that salt air seems to be calling.
It's the one call I cannot deny!
Calling me back to the place I was born,
And the trees where the west winds sigh.

Oh Lord! How I hate all the tinsel!
The blare and the glare of the bars.
The lives that are twisted and wasted,
Weighed down by their honky-tonk scars.

The bustle, the hustle, the hurry,
The dreams that are broken and bent.
The palsied feeling of failure.
The waste of a life, ill spent.

Date Unknown

BIGOTRY

Too long we have judged our fellow man.
We have cried for segregation.
We have forced a hungry multitude,
To live in degradation.

But now! They arise! Their battle cries,
Are heard across the nation.
Their blood has stained our city streets,
In peaceful demonstrations.

In bigotry and selfishness,
The white man seals his doom.
And spirits cry, "Repay. Repay",
From out the moldy tomb!

"I'm thankful, Lord, I'm not as they",
We hear the bigot pray.
"Oh, fool thou art. Thy doom is sealed",
We hear the Master say.

Oh, where is Martin Luther King?
Who said, "We will win at last!"
His blood has stained a dusty road,
By a cowardly shot gun blast.

Why, oh why, can we not live,
As brother unto brother?
For Jesus Christ's commandment was,
That we should love one another.

Date Unknown

WHERE DOES IT END?

When we consider the fleeting stars,
Mercury, Venus, Earth, and Mars,
We also note their orbits planned,
As if placed there by some unseen hand.

For ageless eons, their courses run,
Tied to the "apron strings" of the sun.
Away beyond the Milky Way,
Where Pluto's moons and comets play.

Where Copernicus and Galileo,
On ancient Mars, watched canals grow!
Who sought the secrets of distant stars,
Through shooting showers of meteors.

These learned men have said for years,
There could be fifty-million spheres,
That could shelter life, somewhat like ours,
With birds, and bees, and trees, and flowers.

Should man, therefore, dare to hope,
That beings dwell beyond his scope?
That men somehow, like we, might dwell,
Believing in Heaven, and fearing Hell.

For now, man can only stand and gaze,
And try to pierce that astral haze.
When by some chance, in future days,
He will look beyond the milky ways.

And on some far off planet see,
Another creature, just like me!
Looking back, across the years,
And wondering about, those far off spheres?

March 1975

WHAT IS THIS THING THAT WE CALL SPACE?

What is this thing that we call space,
Where unnumbered planets fly?
Where galaxies we've never seen,
Their allotted courses ply.

What is the force that holds them,
And guides them through the sky?
Untouched, unscathed, unerring,
Where ten-billion others fly!

I find my mind unable,
To understand the things I see,
Or to solve the puzzles hidden,
In this wondrous mystery.

My brain just spins in circles,
As I try to comprehend,
The fact of no beginning,
And certainty of no end.

Are there planets out there,
Able to support the life we know,
With a Heaven up above,
And Hell-fire down below?

How many comets are there,
That come flying at the sun?
Then disappear forever,
When their oblong orbit's done.

Continued...

Who can tell their destination,
As their fiery trail is run,
And they disappear forever,
Out beyond the blazing sun.

Let us picture space encompassed,
On four sides, round about,
With doors that open inward,
And doors that open out.

Just where would you be going,
Should you arrive there some fine day?
And what is your destination,
Should you decide not to stay?

I would ask you please, to tell me,
Who the author might have been,
Of this monumental universe,
And the galaxies therein?

The planets are separated,
By distances so vast,
Before man might reach the nearest one,
Ten lifetimes would have lapsed.

So until mankind is able,
To surpass the speed of light,
He is limited to his planet Earth,
And must accept his plight.

Date Unknown

CHAPTER TWO:

Two Passions ...
History and Nature

A COUNTRY ROAD

You don't think much of a country road,
Does it leads to a humble abode?

But should you get stung by bees from their hive.
Your thoughts are evil along this drive,

And oh! Your thoughts, when you eat the dust!
To have this road fixed, you say, is a must.

At the next council meeting, you always say.
But as usual, this meeting, is months away.

And then the council has bills to pay.
So the road is left for another day.

But we are so thankful for the country road.
Over it have gone wagons, with hay as their load.

Over this road we go to our destination;
The same as our fore-fathers of this great nation.

Along this road there are beauties you can see,
Such as colors so bright in many a tree.

The cattle going home in the day's fading light.
The quiet of this road in the middle of the night.

Don't you hear the music in the croak of the toad?
Can you see the beauty along a Country Road?

Date Unknown

GOD'S COUNTRY

Cascade country, wild and tall,
Land of lakes and waterfalls.

Land of fir trees, towering high,
Land where one knows God is nigh!

Land with cougars on the prowl!
Where hoot owls hoot and coyotes howl.

Land where winter's snow lies deep,
Land where nature's silence keep.

Land where creeks are cold and clear,
Land where one knows God is near.

Where days are warm beneath the sun,
And when He was finished, God said,

"WELL DONE"

August 1972

ODE TO THE PIONEERS

This is a tale of the prairies.
Of pioneers crossing the plains,
Of men who left all, to follow the trails,
Those who left in wagon trains.

Where you honored the code of the west.
You watched the unfit drop by the way.
There's no place for the weakling.
Nature's ruled a billion and one days.

Yes! Wild and wide were the prairies,
Where only the chosen survived.
At times a man, beaten and bent,
Could arise and continue to drive.

Nature! Secretive and selfish,
Waiting ever to catch man off stride.
Where the foolish, the false, and feeble,
Have met her! Then fought her and died.

Like a two-headed goddess she's waiting,
To way-lay the wanton, the weak.
The pallid pimp from the "flesh pots",
Denying them that which they seek.

One by one she betrays and denies them.
She counts as they drop, one by one.
The trail is red from the blood shed,
From Independence to old Oregon.

Continued...

Their quest for land lead them onward.
Staggering, stumbling, and weak!
Forging the turbulent torrent,
Driven onward by that which they seek.

Burning through desert! Short of water.
Counting the oxen that fell.
Cursing the mother that bore them,
Staggering onward through Hell.

Camped at the bend of the river,
Being watched by a brave's burning eyes.
Seeing the arch of the arrows!
Chilled by the screams and the cries.

To freeze, when you feel a "rattler",
Moving ever so slight on your bed.
You then quietly reach for your pistol,
To shoot, and blow off its head.

The West wasn't won by the weaklings!
The sodden, the sick, or the frail,
But by iron-willed men of tempered steel,
Tempered and tried by the trail.

Yes! Strict and stern is the code of the west.
That only the strong may thrive.
The weak and unwilling shall drop by the way,
So the sturdy and staunch might survive.

The dreamers will always be welcome,
Those who visualize things yet to be.
The farms, the firms, and the factories,
Reaching out over this land of the free.

Date Unknown

THE MOJAVE DESERT

What a fascinating place, the desert.
Sage brush and juniper.
A magpie in a joshua tree is scolding.
Heat waves rise,
To disappear into the nothingness from which they came.
And oxen's bones...... lie bleaching.

Sand everywhere.
Yet, here and there a rock peeks out from within the ground.
All at once, a rabbit flees with a leaping bound!
Perhaps in fear, or fright,
Or sheer delight at his own motion!

Then in the sand,
We see small tracks all around that indicate
A band of quail might lie in wait.
Only to depart,
Startling the stillness.

We cannot see or hear
The small beasts and birds that nestle near.
Yet we sense their presence.
For only at night will they appear to search for food.
In mortal fear, they sense the nearness
Of some deadly predator.

Who are we to say the least of these
Is not in his appointed place?
For each must fill his allotted niche
In the manner Mother Nature had decreed.
And in so doing, give to all, that all may live!

Our world will be a better place,
If we but dedicate our lives, to accept it as it is,
And then maintain it
As God expects it to be!

1974

THE NIGHT WIND

I hear the west wind prowling,
Around my house at night,
As I lie awake and listen,
Just waiting for the light.

He rustles at each window.
He rattles at my door.
He howls around my chimney,
And he cools my bedroom floor.

He wrestles with the branches.
I hear the tree tops sigh.
He moans, and groans, and gurgles,
Then for a spell, he's quiet.

One only hopes he's finished.
But then, he goes through,
With a great roar, he comes once more,
Howling down my flue.

He drives the leaves before him.
He roars in fruitless rage.
His ruthless strength is squandered,
Like a lion in a cage.

But in the end he weakens.
We greet a bright, new dawn.
We find a world that's clean and fresh,
And all the smog is gone.

We then greet Mother Nature,
In all her beauty, dressed.
Her cleaning ways, though sometimes rough,
Just have to be the best.

May 1977

JUST A FISHERMAN'S DREAM

Many a tale are told by fishermen bold,
Of the big ones that got away.
And how it tries one's soul,
By the old fishing hole.
And can ruin your whole damn day!

You dream that the chance will come along,
To catch that fish of your dreams.
A fish that will fall,
To the envy of all.
The biggest old fish in the stream!

Well, I saw such a fish in a deep, dark hole,
As I quietly watched one day.
I thought I could see
Him laughing at me,
In a most unsportsmanlike way.

I made a vow, then and there, somehow,
I would have me a fish fillet.
With a fiendish laugh,
I shook my gaff,
As he slowly swam away.

Well, for days I tried, with my flies, hand tied,
Just to prove I was smarter than he.
Why, he was only a fish!
And my fervent wish,
That old fish would be caught by me.

Continued...

Continued...*Just A Fisherman's Dream*

Then I saw him swim slow in that deep, dark hole.
I felt my knees start to knock.
My palms grew wet,
With a nervous sweat,
And my stomach felt like a rock!

But my action was fast, and my rolling cast,
Was as soft as a maiden's kiss.
My aim was sure,
As I watched my lure,
Settle down in that dark abyss.

I watched each cast, as my fly flew fast,
Like a bolt, from a long-bow drawn,
Where the air was still,
With the morning chill,
In the moments just before the dawn.

Then, like a fighting steed with a burst of speed,
He arose to strike my lure.
With a dazzling run,
The fight had begun,
And I had him hooked, I was sure.

I howled with delight as my line grew tight.
My reel screamed with the strain.
As time after time,
He stripped my line,
And I fought him back again.

Continued...

I played that fish like an organist,
With the touch of a master's hand.
While the fight he fought,
Was the fight I sought,
He was the grandest of the grand!

Yes, we fought in the sun, 'til I finally won,
And I scooped him up in my net.
With happy eyes,
I viewed my prize.
He was a champ every way, you can bet!

But wait. Should I keep a fish as noble as this?
He had earned every right to be free!
I retrieved my lure,
And where the water ran pure,
I headed him out to the sea.

Yes, tales are told by fishermen bold,
But not of the ones they set free.
And maybe someday,
As I pass his way,
He'll wave his big tail at me.

September, 1977

NOVEMBER

When sunny days grow shorter,
And the hills have a smoky haze,
When the nights grow long and colder,
And the maples are ablaze.

When Jack Frost stings your fingers,
And your toes are sometimes numb,
You want to snuggle 'neath the covers,
'Cause old November's come.

When mornings are escorted,
By a cold and dreary fog,
Like some nocturnal vision,
Out of an eerie mystic bog.

It's then you prepare for winter,
As you recall the summer sun,
But for now you'll snuggle 'neath the covers,
'Cause old November's come.

You watch the hills grow whiter,
As the snow creeps down the side,
Like a wedding dress, all fluffy,
Worn by a blushing bride.

And then you start in planning,
For the winter holidays,
But for now, you'll snuggle 'neath the covers,
'Cause old November's come.

November 1971

GRANDAD BROOKS

My Grandad Brooks was a pioneer,
And a mountain man to boot.
He crossed the plains with the wagon trains,
Where he learned to ride and to shoot.

He told me tales of the mustang trails,
Where the terrible grizzly growled.
How he'd cock an ear, when the night was clear,
And laughed when the wolf pack howled.

The stories he spun of where he'd been,
Of adventures he'd found here and there.
My blood ran cold when ever he told,
Of being mauled by a Kodiak bear.

He told of his youth, and swore it was truth.
He told of the deserts he'd crossed.
He told of games where the stakes were high,
Of fortunes he'd won and lost.

Of sailing ships, of mutineers,
And of days before the mast,
Of hurricanes in the shipping lanes,
Where he'd swear each day was his last.

Continued...

Continued... *Grandad Brooks*

Of waves as high as a masted ship,
Of winds that ripped and tore,
And of being wrecked where cannibals live,
On a south sea island shore.

Of wars he fought and wounds he got,
Of whining shot and shell,
About Indian wars and terrible scars,
And Indian chiefs who fell.

Then he told of meeting Grandma,
The homestead he claimed in the west,
The cabin he built for his family,
Of a life that was really the best.

I remember that cabin and Grandma,
A most gentle woman, you can bet,
And if you ain't "et" some of her cooking,
Why, brother, you just ain't "et".

I remember her baking soda bread,
When I was just a small boy.
I was lean and hungry with a hollow leg,
And eating her cooking was a joy.

Grandad Brooks is dead now, and gone.
Went to his reward long ago.
I'll never forget my Grandad Brooks,
A fine old man to know

Date Unknown

THEM WERE THE GOOD OLD DAYS

How many times
Have you heard someone say,
They would like to go back
To those "good old days"?
Those good old days,
Away back when.
Women were willing,
And men were men!
Them were the good old days.

Back to the shack,
On the old homestead,
Where, at night, you slept
On a feather bed,
That lay on the floor,
Near the storage bin,
Where that old mother cat,
Had her babies in.
Them were the good old days.

Every morning,
After all were fed,
Grandma saw to it,
The scriptures were read.
There was singing, and praying,
And preaching too,.
(But there were all sorts of things
That I'd rather do.)
Them were the good old days.

Date Unknown

THE CODE OF THE NORTHWEST WOODS

Stern is the code of the Northwest woods.
Tougher still is the logger's code.
For those who ply their logging trade,
Must travel a lonesome road.

For the gods of the logger are calling.
Send me men who have fire in their eye!
Men who will pit their strength against mine,
And before they give up, they will die.

Don't send me the scum from your prisons.
The dregs of the city won't do.
Just send me men who can stand the gaff.
Men who are men, through and through!

Men who are strong for the battle.
Men who are tough to the core.
The weak and the cowardly, I will not accept,
For I wrestle and worry them sore.

For the hand that I brand with, is steady.
The brand that I hold glows red!
Many are they, who bare their chest,
But will pray for death instead!

For tough is the code of the Northwest woods!
Sterner still is the logger's code.
And tough is the man, after facing the brand,
Who can stand up, and carry the load.

November 1977

THE BALLAD OF SASQUATCH

The ad that I read, in the newspaper said,
"The one who could prove beyond doubt,
Would get ten-thousand cash,
To stash in his sash,
For finding where Sasquatch hangs out."

So I figured that I might just as well try,
To find where the Sasquatch roam.
And my brother and I started our quest,
In the Olympics, out west,
That was thought to be Sasquatch's home.

In the mountain tops high, the great glaciers lie,
Covering most of the valleys below.
White glacial ice grips
The granite like a vice,
Made from ten-thousand years of snow.

The crevices abide on the steep mountain side,
To trap any who thoughtlessly go,
Where there's always a chance
That a bad avalanche,
Might smother them all in the snow.

November was spent when we pitched our tent,
Where the giant red cedars grow.
We shivered and shook,
Too frightened to look,
At a thunder and lightning show.

The eerie light that lit up the night,
Seemed to set the mountains aglow.
With each fiery flash,
The thunder's loud crash,
Made the blood in our veins run cold.

Continued...

When the north wind howled, as it poked and prowled,
It seemed like a living thing,
That searched in vain,
Through the sleet and rain,
Which it hurled with a vicious sting.

Through the thunder's quake, we stayed awake,
Too frightened to close our eyes.
We had no doubt,
That Sasquatch was about,
Seeking to take us by surprise!

Where the thunder's flame, with the wind and rain,
Played leap-frog over the hills,
We had little doubt,
That "Old Sas" would come out,
To roam through the mountains, at will.

We looked for a place, he might show his face.
We lived on the food in our packs.
We hunted the trails,
Through valleys and vales,
And we searched in vain for his tracks.

We looked for rifts, in the face of the cliffs.
We scanned each precipice high,
It seemed our quarry,
Could be around the next bend.
We were cursed and caught up in his spell.

We traveled the trails, beat and bent by the gales.
We explored each mountain retreat.
We endured Satan's pain,
As we searched on, in vain,
For the tracks of his over-sized feet.

Continued...

Through the deep winter snows, we damn near froze,
But we'd neither give up nor give in.
We stuck to our guns,
Where the wild rivers run,
While I dreamed of warmer places I'd been.

We searched high and dry. Spring and summer went by,
As winter returned to the scene.
Through each cranny and nook,
We continued to look,
For some place where he might have been.

The squinty-eyed bears, from their mountain lairs,
Watched every move that was made.
Their bristles arose,
In an angry pose,
Making each one of us quite afraid!

To quit, we refused, until at last, our shoes,
Were worn and full of holes.
The snow turned red,
From the blood we shed,
That seeped through our worn-out soles.

Not once in the snow did old Sasquatch show,
Although we sought him for more than a year.
The time that we spent,
Gave me much discontent.
For I know that we never came near.

We covered the ground from Quinault to the Sound,
And I know we will have to give in.
And accept the conclusion,
It's all an elusion.
He's not now, nor has he ever been!

December 1977

OLD "LOKEY" SITS ON THE SIDING

Old "Lokey" sits on the siding.
Her days on the main line are done.
Silent and still she dreams of the thrill,
Of the main lines on which she would run.

The fires that once burned in her boiler,
Like the flame of a new love affair.
No longer ablaze with the passion of youth,
But her memories still linger there.

The rails where she once rolled are rusty.
The bridges she once crossed are burned.
It is sad, when you know you're not needed,
And like a stray dog, you are just spurned.

The headlight that shattered the darkness,
The whistle that moaned through the night,
No longer are parts of the picture,
Seems only to add to her plight.

The passes she passed in the passing of time,
The hobos that once road the rods,
The homeless, the helpless, the knights of the road,
The forgotten, forsaken of God.

Today she resides on the siding.
The days of her doing are done.
The sound of her whistle no longer is heard.
At last she has made her last run.

Date Unknown

THE BIRDS OF PELICAN BAY

The seagulls await at the harbor,
For the boats to return to the shore.
Boats that go out to catch salmon,
Or to capture the albacore.

All day one can hear them complaining,
Competing for each morsel of food.
Loudly they voice their displeasure,
In a manner considered quite rude.

Sharing the bay with the pelicans,
A colony, in numbers, quite large,
Those great graceful birds, which dive for food,
And roost in the bay on a barge.

How graceful, they soar o'er the water,
Where fish, by the millions, survive.
Then when finding one to their liking,
Quickly fold up their wings and dive.

It's amazing, how accurate their aim is!
Very seldom does one ever miss.
It's amusing to see him come up with his catch,
Then watch the gulls get away with his fish.

Oh, how much we humans could profit,
From the pelicans living in peace.
Just how well he gets on with his neighbors,
Would cause most of our troubles to cease.

August 1975

I'VE HUNTED THE TRASK AND THE WILSON

I've hunted the Trask and the Wilson,
Where ridges reach up to the sun.
The brush is as high as an elephant's eye,
And the sneaky coyotes run.

The ridges stand high, reaching upward.
Their peaks penetrating the clouds.
And I've seen when the storm clouds of winter,
Covered each one like a shroud.

I've felled timber up there, when the lightning,
Played tag in the fog, far below.
The lightning's flash! The thunder's crash!
Accompany nature's show!

I've tried in my mind to visualize,
How these hills must have looked before the fire.
A fire that was caused by lust and greed,
In men who were ruled by desire!

Date Unknown

A WORD TO THE WISE

Down through the ages, the poets and sages,
Have written, unending their praise of the west.
They have lauded the fountains, the snow covered mountains,
And our beautiful beaches, with commendable zest.

With poetic oration, they've enlightened the nation,
With pictorial phrases, no one could resist.
They have promised relief, from all of our grief,
And our mental well being, will increase, they insist.

They lay claim to the fixer, that cure-all elixir.
That magical potion, mankind must acquire.
We must all heed their words; take off like the birds,
For this "Garden of Eden", before we expire.

Now, the Oregon coast, no doubt is the toast,
And I'm sure that, we all will agree,
As the scenery unfurls, there's no place in the world,
That has half as much beauty as she.

So from far away places, the populous traces,
The trail ways and trails to our state.
With renewed dedication, they crisscrossed the nation,
Like bears that are lured to the bait.

From the unknown states, they all congregate,
And descend like a covey of quail.
From Crater Lake to Mt. Hood, where camping is good,
They will fill every valley and vale.

Continued…

Continued...*A Word To The Wise*

Our camps on the coast, seem to suffer the most,
As tourists draw a head on the beach.
Then like so many birds, they gather in herds,
And they all seem to stick like a leach.

Tom McCall had a word, for this thundering herd.
"Come to see us, but don't plan to stay.
Spend some 'green', as you take in the scene.
Then pack up, and be on your way."

We love our great trees, where the air's cool and free,
And our lakes, where the fishing is fine.
We don't need a migration, from all over the nation,
So, if you come, stay only a short time.

So, when you make the scene, bring plenty of 'green'.
You will find the Northwest, really swings.
You'll know things are right, from dawn until night,
You can hear a meadow lark sing.

What we'd like to do, is to prove it to you,
That Oregon is a real friendly place.
It's just that we love all the beauty we have
Which puts the big smile on our face.

So, come often, bring the family, and have a good time.
You are as welcome as the flowers of May.
But all good things must come to an end.
So, for goodness sake, don't plan to stay.

June, 1978

I LOVE TO GO OUT CAMPING

I love to go out camping,
Where the water is clear and cold,
Where the air is still, in the morning chill,
And the mountains stand out bold.

The trees all point toward Heaven,
Just as if they are saying "Thanks",
For the beauty that surrounds them,
And the flowers around the banks.

One can hear the breezes humming,
As they wonder through the trees,
And the flowers hang out the "Welcome" sign,
For all the buzzing bees.

Where the dogwood, dressed in their finest,
Seem to smile, as we arrive,
Because, when you go out camping,
It's just great to be alive!

Where the darkness falls too quickly,
As the shadows chase the light,
And the campfires, burning brightly,
Seem to embrace the night.

Where you smell that sweet aroma,
Of the smoldering, campfire coals,
And the water in the nearby creek,
Is bubbling over the shoals.

Where each minute, seems to linger,
As though parting with a friend,
Where we see the night approaching,
And we watch the daylight end.

Where you know no single person,
Contemplates the homeward drive.
'Cause, when you go out camping,
It's just great to be alive.

September 1970

YELLOW GOLD

Have you stood and looked with wonder,
How the Mojave Desert lies?
Where the cactus blooms in splendor,
And at night a coyote cries?

How those heat waves dance before you,
And you watch them as they rise,
Till they disappear, out yonder,
Where the mountains meet the skies.

And you ponder, as you stand there,
Thinking about the days of old,
When the miners trod the ridges,
As they searched for yellow gold.

Where the Indians, riding bareback,
Used to watch the wagon trains,
That were pulled by plodding oxen,
Toward the sunset, across the plains.

Where an oxen's bones lie, bleaching,
Beneath the sagebrush in the sand,
And you wonder, was he slaughtered,
By some hostile Indian band?

While in your mind, an old prospector curses,
As he contemplates his plight.
And he eyes the buzzards soaring,
As they wheel in endless flight.

And again you'll hear him cursing,
All this heat, and dirt, and dust,
And the urge that drives him onward,
Like some unholy trust.

And we dare not, for one moment,
Forget these men of old,
Who helped to build this country,
As they searched for yellow gold.

Date Unknown

THE FATE OF THE WHITE TAIL

Many tales are told, by hunters bold,
Of the deer they have slain in the fall.
Of the trophies they bag,
On side hill or crag,
That hangs in their den, on the wall.

So when the autumn is best, like all the rest,
I head east, where the white tails are fat.
Where hunting is hot,
At my old hunting spot,
Because that's where the big ones are at!

We saw many deer, as we drove here and there,
Scouting the lay of the land.
The season would be open,
At the first crack of dawn,
And we needed to know where to stand.

With the first light of day, we were up and away.
Alert as we walked through the pine.
The ground, as it froze,
Chilled our fingers and toes,
As each sound sent a chill up my spine.

Then, I saw a deer, through the air so clear.
His antlers standing out clear and clean.
As he started to run,
I fired my gun,
But I only hit where he had been.

Continued...

Continued... *The Fate Of The White Tail*

I shot once again, and through the forest I ran.
How I prayed that my aim would be true!
Then I ran to the spot,
Where he'd been when I shot.
I found my bullet, his shoulder, passed through!

My breath came in gasps, from running so fast,
To the place where he laid on the ground.
I marveled indeed,
At the white tail breed,
And the antlers, he wore for a crown.

I watched his eyes glaze, and I continued to gaze,
At this beautiful beast at my feet.
I thought of all the steak,
That his carcass would make,
As well as the rest of the meat.

I'm sure that each one has his life span to run,
And is destined to meet with his fate.
Who if any, can say,
That it's wrong today,
For this deer to end up on my plate.

And though a tear came to my eye, as I watched that deer die,
I'm sure that it was meant to be thus.
That the deer were destined,
To be food for men.
Why, then, should so few make a fuss?

October 1977

56

I'VE STOOD AMONG THE MOUNTAINS

I've stood among the mountains,
Where the Olympics' mighty spires,
Have spawned the booming thunder,
And set the lightning fires.

It's there I've felt the presence,
Of forces, far beyond,
The mind of men to comprehend,
And unable to respond.

In awe and wonder I have noted,
All the beauty that is there.
The mountains reaching, ever upward,
Upward, to God knows where.

I can hear the thunder growling,
As it wrestles with the peaks,
And the quietness is shattered,
When the streaking lightning speaks.

The glaciers unrelenting,
Ride the mountains, "piggy-back",
In a silence so over-powering,
That one fears one's mind might crack.

Amid Olympic Mountains,
Dwelt the Indian's Thunderbird,
Whose eyes flashed bolts of lightning,
And in who's voice, was thunder heard!

Date Unknown

WINTER TIME

It's winter time! The skies are gray.
The sun is pale. How short the days,
And all the leaves are gone.

The trees are bare, the branches nude.
The hungry birds still search for food.
And finally find, there is none!

Winter time! The nights are chilled.
The full moon rises above the hill,
And goes away when day is born.

When winter winds are on the prowl,
And you think you hear an old wolf howl,
As if to show his scorn.

Winter time! The winds blow cold!
The days grow short. The sun sets gold.
And the snow prepares to enter.

Holidays are in the air.
Menus planned for festive fare.
And a turkey gobbles his displeasure.

Winter time! The sky is gray.
And darkness comes while it's still day.
And street lights gleam, before their time.

Winter time! At last, his song is sung.
The grass shows green. The days grow long.
And winter has outworn his stay.

And he is through! Chased far away,
By spring, who plans to stay.
Or so we hope it's true!

October 1970

WORKING ON
THE YARDER SIDE

In memory, I see a "yarder",
On a hillside far away.
And it seems she's over anxious,
Just to start another day.

I can hear her whistle blowing,
Saying to the crew, "Let's go."
As the logs head for the landing,
Where the big trees used to grow.

The crew is ever willing,
To put their shoulder to the wheel.
Grab that choker while she's swinging.
Buckle up that "ball of steel".

Stand aside. Then blow that whistle.
Send that turn into the tree.
Then to the mill and into lumber,
To build homes for you and me.

Back again with rigging screaming!
Chokers flying high and wide.
Got to get them logs to market,
Working on the "high ball" side.

The "hooker", watchful, eyes the action,
As his rigger "splices twine".
Splicing "eyes", into the "haywire",
To transfer the "haul back" line.

Continued…

Half the tree is logged now.
Swing the "blocks", and change the "load".
Call the "climber", swing the "bull block".
Got to get those trucks a load.

So it goes, day after day.
That old "spar tree", a 'swaying,
As rigging whistles fill the air,
Their messages conveying.

The "loading donkey" does her thing.
She sits with "tongs" a 'flying,
With "guy lines" strung, a "squirrel block" hung,
And a "heel boom" proudly plying.

"Head loaders" have to know their stuff.
The "second loaders" too,
For all the loads must balance, just so,
No other way will do.

So it goes from day to day.
A logger flirts with danger.
To winter storms and summer heat,
Believe me, he's no stranger.

Yes, a logger's life is a brutal life.
He works in rugged places.
Not many people, a logger would be,
If they knew of the danger he faces.

January 1978

IN MY GARDEN GROW SOME ROSES

In my garden grow some roses,
Their fragrance fills the air.
My life I find, much more fulfilled,
Just to have them there.

Their beauty lights the morning,
They nod as I go by,
They sway like dancers dancing,
Beneath a cloudless sky.

They brighten up my entire yard,
With yellows, pinks, and reds,
They are the flowers that lovers send,
And mourners use for the dead.

Man with all his "know-how",
Finds he simply can't compete,
Should he try to copy nature,
He is doomed to dull defeat.

For only nature knows the secret,
Of what it takes to make a rose.
A thing of beauty to the eye,
A joy unto the nose.

Date Unknown

I REMEMBER, OH, SO WELL

I remember, oh, so well,
How my granddad used to tell,
About those good old days,
Because he was there.
How they crossed the rolling plains,
With their plodding oxen trains,
And there wasn't a road,
Or signboard anywhere.

Well, times were plenty tough,
When they loaded up their stuff,
And they left their friends behind,
And headed west.
But in God, they put their trust,
As they prayed, that He'd be just,
And they swore that they would make it,
Or they'd bust.

But in spite of all their ills,
They kept on heading for them hills,
'Cause some one told them, way out yonder,
There was gold.
So with visions of those riches,
They just kept hitching up their britches,
As, heading toward the sunset,
They watched their wagons roll.

Date Unknown

WHEN THE LEAVES ARE TURNING GOLD

Have you ever gone out hunting,
When the leaves are turning gold?
Where the frost makes white the countryside,
When the nights are getting cold?

Where the aspens are a 'quiver,
As they dance in golden dress,
And the snow lies like a mantle,
Over the mountain wilderness.

Where maples in their glory,
Like a symphony untold,
Of orange, and green, and scarlet,
And hues of yellow gold.

Nature donned them in their finest,
For these last few fleeting days,
As they prepare to meet the winter,
Foretold by autumn haze.

While the does are shyly flirting,
the bucks are getting bold.
Don't you love to go out hunting,
When the leaves are turning gold?

Continued...

You can see a big moon shining.
And you hear a coyote cry,
While you sit around the campfire,
Underneath a starlit sky.

You watch the sparks fly upwards,
Pursued by swirling smoke.
You think about the coming day,
And give the fire a poke.

As once again with hunting pals,
You hear old stories told,
From those who go out hunting,
When the leaves are turning gold.

And then you find you're lulled to sleep,
By a softly sighing breeze,
That sings the night song of the eve,
As it moves among the trees.

It's then you know for certain,
As these mysteries unfold,
It's just great to be out hunting,
When the leaves are turning gold.

October 1974

TODAY WE STAND AT THE CROSS ROAD

Today we stand at the cross road.
We seek the direction we need.
We spend our time seeking answers,
From people who pay us no heed.

Our economy seems to be shaken.
Interest has gone out of sight.
Unemployment is growing by leaps and bounds.
Why a man can't sleep at night.

Our nation must have a new leader.
Carter's made too many mistakes.
Anderson can't seem to get going,
And Reagan aint got what it takes.

Right now we have the three "Stooges",
Like Curly, Larry and Moe.
With Ronny, Jimmy and Georgie,
Which way is a man supposed to go?

The Iranians are holding us hostage.
The Russians are building the bomb.
The Arabs are fighting each other,
So who knows what is liable to come.

Continued...

Here at home there is shooting and killing.
On the streets there is robbing and rape.
The hoodlums are mugging and mauling.
There seems little chance for escape.

It seems that nature's against us.
Fires and earthquakes all around!
People are dying by thousands!
Yet no reason can really be found.

I ask you, my brother, pray tell me.
Just what does the future hold?
Are the treasures we manfully sought for
Turning into fool's gold?

Americans ever are worthy.
They will never give out, or give in.
It is a known fact they will come back fighting,
After taking one to the chin.

So regardless of who wins the elections,
We will ever stand like steel.
When trouble comes, we'll all be ready,
To put a shoulder to the wheel.

September 1980

YUKON TRAIL

My grandad told of his search for gold,
In the rush of ninety-eight.
He told of camps in the frozen north,
And of miners who couldn't wait.

He told of women, who followed the camps,
Wanton, painted, and pale,
Of miners who paid with hard-earned gold,
Dug on the Yukon Trail.

Where the gray wolf howled at the polar moon,
Beneath the spires of the distant hills.
Where night after night, the northern lights,
Flashed with a glory that chills.

He told how the spell seemed to hold him;
How he sought and fought for the lode.
Of toil and sweat in the killing cold,
And he swore that he'd pay what he owed.

Where the merciless cold seemed to make the gold;
An evil you'd like to forget.
And you curse the day you found your way
To the land where the sun never sets.

Continued...

He told of the man-killing Chilkoot Pass;
Of men who floundered and failed,
Of the hopes and dreams lost in the streams
That were part of the Yukon Trail.

Of the weary men that he met there;
Of the few he learned to call friend.
He spoke of the days and the various ways,
He was beaten and broke in the end.

Of the few who found a fortune
In the unfriendly valleys and vales.
And the many found frozen to death
Beside the old Yukon Trail.

He told how the gold, at last petered out,
How they traveled trails leading to Nome,
In loneliness roamed in the Arctic cold,
Deciding at last, to go home.

And he says he's going to go back someday,
To the valleys and vales where he toiled,
To the North Country, ever encompassed by cold,
And the Yukon, forever, unspoiled.

Date Unknown

THE TREASURE OF NEAKANIE

Come listen while I tell you of treasure.
Treasure that's hid 'neath the sand.
Treasure from the Inca's own storehouse.
Fought for and died for, by man.

Gold! That's been sought for by thousands.
Silver! Like you never have seen.
Riches beyond comprehension.
Riches where no riches had been.

Borne by a ship from Grenada,
Blown far off its course in a gale.
Gored by the rocks off Neakanie!
Shorn, by the wind of its sail.

The ship! An old Spanish galleon.
Plying the old Spanish Main!
Sacking the towns of the Incas!
From the sea shore, way up 'cross the plain.

Raiding, raping and plunder,
Gold! For the courts of old Spain.
Gold! The glory that was once Grenada,
Might be seen by the world, once again.

Caught in a gale from the southward.
Fleeing north to escape the high seas.
Meeting her doom at the headland,
Beaten and brought to her knees.

All battered and bashed by the breakers,
With no hope that she'd ever sail more.
The captain and crew, with the treasure,
Forsook her and took for the shore.

Continued...

It was here that they buried the treasure!
Deep down in a dark mountain cave,
To discourage the natives from taking the chest,
They murdered and buried a slave.

They were watched by the natives, in hiding,
As the chests were placed deep in the sand,
And perhaps, could do nothing but wonder,
About these men from some far away land.

Now the tale still prevails that all perished.
One by one, they were slain, on the beach,
Leaving the treasure to lure men on,
A vision, that's just out of reach.

Yet another rumor prevailing,
Tells of one of the Spaniards who hid,
And lived to recover the treasure.
There are those who say that he did.

And then those who maintain the treasure,
Still lies on the mountain's south slope.
And many a man has strived and lost,
And left, bereft of all hope.

The hope that it's out there, just waiting,
Is enough to drive strong men to drink.
And the hard work demanded of searching,
Has left some unable to think.

But man is ever a dreamer.
And can only be sure that he'll die!
He'll take his last breath while searching,
For the treasure on Mt. Neakanie.

June 1974

ARIZONA

Arizona? Yes, I've been there.
Where the mountains reach the sun.
Where the desert goes forever,
And the old road runner runs.

The color of the canyons,
More than match the rainbow hues.
It's no wonder Arizonians,
Never seem to have the blues.

No matter where you travel,
North, or south, or east, or west.
Each new vista that confronts you,
Has to be the very best.

Grand Canyon is breath-taking,
In fact, it's beyond belief.
No matter how long you plan to stay,
Your visit is too brief.

That magic, mystic something,
Where the superstitions rise,
Leaves one weak and empty-headed,
When at night a coyote cries.

One can but only wonder,
As he hears the stories told,
Of the Superstition Mountains,
Or the Dutchman and his gold.

Date Unknown

WHEN THE MAPLES TURN TO SCARLET

When the wild geese, winging southward,
Send their cries across the land,
It's then I think of hunting,
Where the ponderosa stand.

Where the does are getting watchful,
As the bucks are getting bold,
When the maples turn to scarlet,
And the aspens turn to gold.

The mountain sides are changing,
From brown to golden tan,
The sage has ceased it's blooming,
Where the long-eared rabbits ran.

When the summer days grow shorter,
When the autumn nights grow cold,
When maples change to scarlet,
And the aspens change to gold.

Where the campfire smoke trails upward,
And the fire has a welcome feel,
When the stories told, 'round the campfire,
Seem almost to be real.

When the trail, with frost a 'glitter,
And your toes grown numb with cold.
When the maples turn to scarlet,
And the aspens turn to gold.

October 1978

JUST TRAVELING

I raised my family when times were tough.
I never could seem to get enough,
Of that folding green to pay all of my bills.
The only thing I knew how to do,
Was cutting trees on a cutting crew,
Or bucking logs, away back in them hills.

Why, I'd been married, for thirty years,
Amid working and sweating and shedding tears,
Before I ever had a dime to call my own,
It seemed to me, that we moved a lot,
From camp to camp and from spot to spot,
Like a hungry dog, I searched for a bigger bone.

I soon found that to play this game,
One had to win, or go insane,
Cause my frustrations just had to have a vent.
Since we liked to hunt, and camp, and fish,
We figured a trailer would be our dish,
And it ain't much fun, caught in a rain storm, in a tent.

A friend of mine had one, "home-made".
It was really quite small, but the license was paid.
And for $200.00, he was willing to sell.
It wasn't long, after that, we found out,
We needed something bigger, to get about,
And we wanted a toilet that didn't smell.

Well, it's a fact, that we have had four.
We pulled them twenty-thousand miles or more,
And I tell you, we have seen a lot of sights.
We have been where the cowboys rode the trail,
Where the "Pony Express" packed the mail,
And we gambled beneath them gaudy, Reno lights.

Continued...

We have seen Indians in their barren land,
And deserts, where the shifting sand,
Moved like a living thing.
We saw Indian women selling beads,
That they had made from cedar seeds,
And we heard a Rocky Mountain canary sing.

In awe, we saw Grand Canyon's sweep,
In silence stood, where the ancients sleep.
We saw the houses made from stone.
In a land unfriendly, hostile and hard,
We saw the cacti standing guard,
So still, so stiff, so stately, all alone.

Now, if you ain't been there, you ought to go.
Get away from it all, where there ain't no snow,
And there is an awfully lot to see.
Get that load off of your back.
Pack your camper and hit the track,
And see just how good it feels, to just be free!

Now, I tell you, friend, whether you like it or not,
When you find yourself in that graveyard plot,
You're going to be there a good, long spell.
Why not relax, while the going's good,
And do the things that you know you should?
And tell that "Old Grim Reaper" to go to Hell.

June, 1977

AN AUTUMN LOVE AFFAIR

The days of Indian summer,
That linger on the autumn haze.
The grain that once was dressed green,
Is now gold and amber blaze.

The leaves that once clad all the trees,
When autumn winds are blown,
In one last fling, they flaunt their love,
As their wild oats are sown.

For this last fling, they dress their best,
In gowns of red and brown.
And in passion, cling to passing winds,
Who find their panties down.

Where, shamelessly, they nestle,
For one last long embrace.
And in my pansy bed they find,
Their final resting place.

But they're not satisfied with this.
From bed to bed they're hopping,
As through the air, their love affair,
Continues without stopping.

At last they cease, and find release,
From their unstated yearning,
And to the skies their spirits rise,
In sacrificial burning.

February 1975

THE SEA BUG

I was born where the sound of the roaring surf,
Like a lullaby, lulled me to sleep.
For all of my life, I've been bit by that bug,
And I guess that she's got me for keeps.

When you're bit by that bug, you're a goner!
It is then you belong to the sea.
You will be in love with the ocean forever,
And from her you can never be free.

What a thrill! Just to stroll through the driftwood.
Maybe find a glass float from Japan,
A tropical treasure from some far away isle,
Or a note from some cast-away man!

Just to sit, quietly watching the water,
As it comes and goes, never still.
Unceasing, she grinds at the headlands,
Like grain that is ground in the mill.

For, from moment to moment, she changes,
But its beauty is ever the same.
One moment she roars like a lion.
The next she is pussy cat tame.

Like a woman, you can't take her for granted!
Like a woman, she'll lead you astray.
She's a fickle and two-timing lover,
And forever she'll have her own way.

August 1975

THE NORTH LAND

There's a land that lies up northward.
A land where the rivers run free.
A land where the salmon are spawning.
And oh, how it beckons me.

The rivers run free and they sparkle.
They are wild as they rush through the glen.
Untamed, unchained, and unyielding,
They refuse to be conquered by men.

There are lakes like the jewels in a setting.
Only God can say where they lie.
Reflecting the beauty of Heaven,
And light from the stars in the sky.

Lakes where the rainbows are rising.
Where an eagle, on motionless wings,
Glides over the lake in the morning,
Where the jay and the whippoorwills sings.

The mountains reach upward toward Heaven.
Snow-laden, the footstools of God.
Dressed in their ermine-white mantle.
Denying the spawn of the sod.

Holding back man from the summits.
Denying the treasures they seek.
Defeating their every effort.
Leaving them battered and weak.

Continued…

Continued... *The North Land*

Mountains that seem to reach Heaven,
Holding valleys where men never trod.
Relentless, unyielding, unconquered,
Reflecting the spirit of God.

Oh, how they stand out, alluring.
Seductive, they keep calling me on.
Like a woman, they promise all that you seek,
Then leaves you weak, come the dawn.

Those mountain peaks, shining and silent,
Attractive, alluring and mean,
Summoning men to their altars,
Where they fade like a nightmarish dream.

It seems that men become helpless,
Whenever a snowcap may loom,
Leaving their homes and their loved ones,
To face the deadfalls and dooms.

Wherever the avalanche threatens,
And the crevices gape for their bones,
The untrained, the weak, and weary,
Come where the mountain wind moans.

But oh, how their beauty enthralls me.
It seems to bring me closer to God.
We are held in their spell till our dying day,
And are lain to rest 'neath the sod.

1980

DRIVING SOUTH ALONG THE COAST

Driving south along the coast,
When a southwest storm is blowing.
Watching surf, and sea, and sand,
Not caring where we're going!

Rain bound ridges quickly pass.
Somewhere, a seagull's calling,
As out beyond the jetty's end,
We hear a fog-horn bawling.

The great rocks stand along the shore,
Like guardians of the deep,
From age to age they calmly stand,
Their lonely vigils keep.

Now, there is no place, upon the face
Of this old world, I'm knowing,
That can compare with the Oregon coast,
When a southwest storm is blowing!

August 1975

WE DROVE
THE MIGHTY ROGUE

We drove the Rogue to Agness,
On a rainy August day.
Over the ridges, through the valleys,
Where the gloomy rain clouds lay.

The autumn leaves were falling.
All yellow, brown, and red,
They nestled beneath the myrtles,
Along the river bed.

We saw a fawn deer feeding,
The grass was deep and lush,
He quickly moved on tiny legs,
And vanished in the brush.

We watched the fishermen fishing,
As we drove along the way,
Below the rushing rapids,
Where the fighting steelhead lay.

We marveled at the berries,
Hanging ripe, and thick, and sweet.
So good for pies and jellies,
Just grand to stop and eat.

Stopping at Lucas Ranch House.
They serve dinner, family style.
With good old family cooking,
Taking seconds, makes you smile.

Then on home, along the north bank.
The wipers beating time to the rain.
What a beautiful river to travel.
And I'll do it again, it is plain.

August 1975

GETTING CAUGHT IN A JULY SQUALL

For days and days we trolled the waves,
Where the fighting coho calls,
Away to the west, where the combers crest,
And the fog-bound buoy bawls.

The sky was as blue as a maiden's eyes.
The wind came in from the south.
Our boat slid through the rolling sea,
As we left the Chetco's mouth.

Beyond the bar, like a piece of glass,
The sea lay smooth and flat,
As above the ridge, away to the east,
A summer sunrise sat.

The sun rose fast as we left port.
The wind was a gentle breeze.
While over the city, the fog hung low,
Hiding all, but the tops of the trees.

Our poles were rigged with a herring jig,
As we headed west of south,
Where the pelicans fly and seagulls cry,
Away out from the Windchuck's mouth.

Then out of the south, the wind picked up.
The spray began to fly.
From a sea that was calm, a moment ago,
Came rollers nine feet high!

Continued...

Like water bugs, the small boats fled!
Trying to make it to shore,
As rain came down in torrents,
And the wind began to roar.

Now I was sure, that a storm like this,
Was not the place for me.
So we pulled our lines and headed home,
Through the steadily mounting sea.

All, save one, made the harbor's mouth,
Through the steadily mounting sea.
And many a prayer was gratefully said,
For arriving there, safely.

Out of one hundred and seventy-eight boats,
One alone was lost!
When down by Bird Island, a cruiser,
Upon the rocks, was tossed.

All the people were saved by the Coast Guard,
But they lost their boat and the gear.
But, come tomorrow, they'll be fishing again,
For the fishing fold is a breed, without fear.

Yes, those fishing folk quite soon forget,
As out to the ocean they go.
How quickly a calm and quiet sea,
Can change into a July blow.

August 1975

CHAPTER THREE:

The Near and Dear

WHEN YOU WERE A LITTLE GIRL

When you were a little girl,
A long time ago,
You would bump your head,
Or stub your toe.
I would gather you up,
And hold you tight,
Just to let you know
Things would be alright.

You would snuggle down.
I would wipe your nose.
Then I'd kiss the spot,
That hurt the most.
Oh, it wouldn't be long,
Till a smile was there.
The tears would be gone,
Because you knew I cared.

Today, how I'd love
To do the same.
To dry your tears,
To ease the pain,
To let you know
As I hold you tight,
That things just got
To turn out right.

I want you to know,
That we love you, Dear.
So please hurry home,
Because we are waiting here.
And one more time,
I will hold you tight.
Just to let you know
Things will turn out right.

May 1986

BIMMY, A LITTLE DOG

Man's best friend is a dog, I've been told,
And I'm sure that it has to be true.
You don't need a dog with a long pedigree.
Just any old hound dog will do!

I had such a dog, called him Bimmy.
A poodle that almost could talk.
He loved to go with us, to ride in the car,
Or if we just left the house for a walk.

Bimmy learned fast and I taught him,
To retrieve a ball when I wanted him to.
He was eager to do what I wanted,
And he loved to show off what he knew.

Poor Old Bimmy got sick, and I took him
To the clinic, to get him a shot.
I knew he was ailing and "sick as a dog",
Because his body was feeling so hot.

The last time I saw him alive,
The nurse took him away and I cried.
With his big brown eyes, he seemed to say,
"I just want to be by your side."

Old Bimmy's been gone for five or six years,
But I still think of him now and then.
There's a place in my heart that will ever be his.
My old dog, my buddy, my friend.

If dogs have a heaven, I'm certain,
Old Bimmy will be in the front row.
There must be a place for the good dogs that die,
And I'm sure that's where Bimmy would go!

November 1975

BONNIE HAS A PUSSY CAT

Bonnie has a pussy cat.
He weighs about a ton.
His fur is thick. His feet are white,
And he is lots of fun.

He doesn't know that he's a cat!
He eats just like a hog.
He always runs to meet her car,
And acts just like a dog.

When first he came,
He seemed a wee bit scrawny.
His nose was black. His ears were black,
While in between he's tawny.

His tail is like a flaunted plume.
He carries it so proudly,
And shows his love for your attention,
By purring, oh, so loudly!

Date Unknown

CHILDREN

Active children,
Noisy children,
Learning ABCs,
All about the birds and bees,
How the fly walks up the wall.
Why he doesn't fall at all?
Children

Laughing children,
Happy children,
Learning that the world is round.
Why it's up, when we are down.
Why two and two is always four.
(Rabbits sometimes make it more.)
Children

Chubby children,
Skinny children,
We learn at times that they're lethargic.
Boys to spinach are allergic.
Girls with lips and eyes, so pretty,
Smiling, flirting, and looking pretty.
Children

(I guess we learn from children.)

Date Unknown

GOBBIES

One day as I sat in the sunshine,
Katie Kid, sat by my side.
"How much do you love me?" I asked her.
"Whole GOBBIES," she replied.

"How much", you may ask, "is a GOBBIE?"
Why, everyone knows, good and well,
That each fairy must carry a GOBBIE,
But, just what it is, they'll not tell!

Why, the fairies, will all use a GOBBIE,
To measure the love that I see in her eyes.
And to count all the stars that the angels,
Hung up in the soft evening skies.

It would take a whole bunch of GOBBIES,
With each one, filled good and tight,
To hold the love that I feel in her arms,
When she hugs me, to kiss me goodnight!

Why, a GOBBIE is made, just for measuring love!
They are the "onliest" thing that will do.
To fathom the love, in a little girl's heart,
When she says, "Grampa, I love you!"

February 1974

I'M REFERRIN' TO MY MA

Who has eyes that sparkle, like the stars that shine at night?
Who has cheeks so pink and rosy, who smiles with all her might?

Who has a word of kindness, when the going seems too tough?
Who dishes out encouragement, when everything seems rough?

Who is the grandest person, anybody ever saw?
Why, everybody knows that I'm referrin' to my Ma.

Who sacrificed for me, when I was just a kid?
Who overlooked my meanness, and the ornery things I did?

Who went without to buy me, skates, or let me see a show?
Who held me tight when I was hurt, because she loved me so?

Who, like a lovely diamond, doesn't have a single flaw?
Why, everybody knows that I'm referrin' to my Ma.

Whose hair is touched with grey now? Whose eyes are just as
bright?
Who prays with reverence, when she retires at night?

Who has a word of kindness, for everyone she sees?
Who loves what God have given us; the birds, the flowers, the
trees?

Who doesn't have an enemy, who honors every law?
Do you wonder that we love her? I'm referrin' to my Ma.

Date Unknown

MY HOME

I dream of my home and my loved ones.
A home that meant ever so much.
Of holidays and happy times,
On Christmas, and Easter, and such.

I can still hear my boy's joyous laughter,
As he listened to a radio show,
Or how excited he used to get,
When he saw the new fallen snow.

I recall a little boy smiling,
As he played on the floor with delight.
I still feel his arms as he held me,
To hug me, and kiss me goodnight.

I dream of my girls, both grown now,
Of the joys and tears that are past.
Of the good times we had when together,
And the years flying by, too fast.

I think of the girl that I married,
And how much we still are in love.
I hope that it might last forever,
With God's blessings sent from above.

She has made our house a home, my friend,
With quiet, loving care.
You will find no ill will or quarreling,
Because love is living there!

1974

TO MY FAVORITE WIFE

Of all the women I have seen,
Within this vale of tears,
Short ones, fat ones, tall ones,
And those way up in years.

Skinny ones, lean ones, ugly ones,
Ones with looks and without.
With false teeth, false hair, false love.
Buck teeth and a nose like a snout.

Bow legged, skinny legged,
And those with knees that knock,
Gentle ones, clingy-vine ones.
Some who are hard as a rock.

I've looked the whole crew over,
And you can bet I've got a hunch.
I wouldn't trade my one sweet wife,
For any of the bunch.

"PAPPY"

Date Unknown

GOD'S LITTLE ANGEL

When the good Lord made the angels,
And taught them how to sing,
It seems he had one angel,
Who hadn't any wings.

Dressed in gossamer, moonlit lovely!
Face so child-like, smiling bright.
But what could God do, with an angel,
Who had no wings for flight?

So God pondered, long and lonely,
O'er this lonely, wingless sprite.
What could he do to make things better,
To change this wrong to right?

He could keep her, there in Heaven,
To improve that wondrous dome,
Or make of her a mother,
And send her to our home.

So thus, I found God's angel!
When she chose to be my bride.
To be the mother of my children,
To walk with me, side by side.

And I shall evermore be grateful,
And to God, I will confess,
This angel, born without her wings,
Invented happiness.

April 1975

TO MY WIFE BEA

For 41 years, through work, sweat, and tears,
Through depressions, through good times and bad,
My sweet wife, Bea, has put up with me.
She's the best wife a man ever had.

We were married quite young, and I know there were some,
Who said that a marriage like ours, couldn't last.
But we hung on real tight, never once had a fight,
And laughed as we watched the years pass.

It hasn't been easy, nor has it been smooth,
But it's never been dull, you can bet.
She always is waiting for me to come home!
She's my darling, my sweetheart, my pet.

My house is my castle, and my little wife,
Tells me that I am the Boss!
Sometimes, when I'm fishing, and I'm late getting home,
She never, ever, gets cross.

So now, I know, if I'm careful, and live by the book.
And things keep on being nifty,
By the Grace of the Lord and a good tailwind,
It should not be hard to reach 50!

October 1970

REMEMBERING THE GOOD TIMES

It seems, as I grow older,
That my feet keep getting colder.
The hair upon my head is getting thin.
    I find the news print getting dimmer.
    The situation's grimmer,
When I sometimes can't remember where I've been.

Still, I remember now and then,
Those good times, a way back when,
The girls flocked around me by the score.
    There was Rosa, dark and pretty.
    There was Wanda, warm and witty.
How I'd like to have those good old days once more.

Though I brag not what I am,
You can bet I was the man,
That filled their hum-drum lives with sheer delight!
    But things got complicated,
    As they stood in line and waited.
It seemed, they had me cornered, day and night.

It was then I made my mind up,
I sure wasn't going to wind up,
Before that altar, with a ring stuck in my nose.
    So, to keep my single bliss,
    I would just have to keep them "miss",
Which meant I must stay awake, and on my toes.

But it finally wore me down.
A little "Bea" with eyes of brown,
Finally stung me with that fatal sting!
    Before I knew what really mattered,
    I was walking to the altar,
Where I put upon her hand, a golden ring.

That's been fifty years ago, but still
There's one thing I would like to know.
Without me, how could all those gals survive?
    I guess, I'll never know,
    Because my age has made me slow,
And I find, I have a narrow-minded wife!
    (She never would let me chase girls!)

December 1970

CHAPTER FOUR:

A Different Side

THE PRIVY THAT MY GRANDAD USED TO HAVE

I remember that old 'privy',
That sat on Grandad's farm,
Where the facts of life were pondered,
Within it's simple charm.

The door, with leather hinges,
Gave the privacy one sought,
From the prying eyes of neighbors,
Who watched, but all for naught.

Just to sit in meditation,
And watch a spider, as she spun,
Let the reverie surround you,
As ten-thousand insects hum.

And if you weren't in any hurry,
You could browse the catalogue,
Where they sold those ladies 'undies',
Or a collar for your dog.

The trail leads through the orchard,
Out behind the apple tree.
Should you ever really need it,
Sure was a welcome sight to see.

I won't forget that doorway,
Standing silently, ajar,
Had a "Welcome" sign upon it,
With a new moon, and a star.

Continued...

Continued...The Privy That My Grandad Used To Have

Yes, the memories surround me,
Of the "outhouse" on the hill,
And those nostalgic recollections,
That come and go at will!

It seems to me that privy,
Bore the brunt of spirit's spleen,
By being laid out horizontal,
Almost every Halloween.

I recall my dear Aunt Lizzie,
Who, in meditation, sat,
When the ghosts and goblins ascended,
Leaving what she sat on, flat!

While old Aunt Lizzie, on the inside,
Was shouting, "Help me, please, someone!"
Those ghosts were on the ground,
A 'rolling and laughing at the fun.

For in falling, that old privy,
Had landed on its door,
And Aunt Lizzie, raged and rabid,
Was trapped for an hour or more.

Yes! I remember that old privy,
That sat on Grandad's farm.
Where the facts of life were pondered,
Within it's rustic charm.

January 1978

HOW I STOLE A BELL AND GOT CAUGHT

I grew up in a hard luck family,
That had nine healthy kids.
And it seems like only yesterday,
That we did the things we did.

Once, when we lived up the Santiam,
Where the fir trees grow straight and tall.
The air was clear and cleaner then,
It seems, as I recall.

The ridges that surrounded us,
Seemed to almost reach the sky,
To get in the way, where the red hawks play,
And the great bald eagles fly.

With our old dog "Scout", we roamed about,
Enjoying the sights and the sounds,
For there wasn't much trouble a boy could get into,
In that little old one-horse town.

Yet, I would agree, between you and me,
There were places where we left our mark.
There are people today, who are premature gray,
Because of some of our lark.

One was a neighbor, who had a donkey, name "Jake",
On whose neck hung a bell of brass.
That would loudly ring out as old Jake walked about,
So this neighbor could find his own ass.

So I, like any kid, might have done,
Took a shine, to that old brass bell,
Thereby, becoming all mixed up in sin,
As I walked down that pathway toward hell.

Continued...

Or so, I was later led to believe,
When my ma found out what I'd done.
And I can still hear her say, how sorry she was,
To have a thief for a son.

Well, inside plumbing had not yet caught on,
And everyone's "John" was outside.
Where the odoriferous aroma permeated the air,
Would lead one to believe, John had died.

There were three holes in the seat where we sat.
A catalogue nailed to the wall,
In which, without care, we would pass the hardware,
And reach women's "undies" by fall.

But, let us get back, to the pertinent facts,
Concerning that old bell of brass.
When giving into temptation, in a moment of weakness,
I stole from the neck of an ass.

Under cover of darkness, where no light penetrated,
I secretly hid that old bell,
Behind our old "Ky-Bo" where spider webs stand,
And all kinds of cockroaches dwell.

Well, it didn't take long, for things to calm down,
And soon things, once again, were serene.
I had the brass bell, and all seemed to be well,
Until Ma walked in on the following scene.

One day, as we played, the way boys will play,
Out back behind our smelly old "John",
I said to old Chuck, "There's a bell back there.
You go in there, and bring it out, son."

Continued...

But Chuck wouldn't move; he just stood there.
I got mad, and started to swear.
He says, "I'm not going in after that bell,
'Cause there are spiders and cockroaches there."

I still tried to tell him, in spite of his fears,
That all would turn out quite well.
But good old Chuck just stood there, and told me,
Real quick, that I could go straight to hell!

In a moment or two, Ma hears all the fuss.
She came out, breathing fire and smoke.
She stood there, arms 'a'kim-bo',
She sized things up before she spoke.

"Now boys, come here and listen.
There is one thing I would like to know,
How did the bell of brass, from our neighbor's ass,
Get behind our old Ky-Bo?"

Then, word by word, the awful truth,
Chuck spouted out, to seal my doom.
'Twas then and there, Ma she grabbed me,
And began to beat me with her broom.

"Good old Chuck" just stood there,
While Ma whacked and whaled away.
'Till finally out of breath, she said,
"I hope you'll mend your ways."

And so my friends, my story ends,
About that bell of brass,
And when Mother made me, put it back
Upon my neighbor's ass.

March 1975

ODE TO THE WOODPECKER

Of all the birds that ever was,
I like the woodpecker best, because
Although he pecks forever more,
His little pecker don't get sore!

He spends his time amid the trees,
Pecking for worms, and bugs, and bees.
Though he pecks with all his might,
His little pecker stays quite tight.

We watch him as he pecks with ease,
Leaving holes in all the trees.
Now won't one think his mind is weak,
From all the beating with his beak?

It's not hard to understand,
As he goes pecking 'cross the land,
Why, there's anger in the people,
Because he's pecked upon their steeple.

So, when we hear him on a church,
Or anywhere that he may perch,
We know just why he pecks on wood.
It makes his pecker feel so good.

Date Unknown

HOW I LEARNED THE LOGGING TRADE

I left home, when but a lad,
To work in the woods with my old dad,
And I soon found out that I didn't know very much.
We headed out where the trees grow tall,
Where I soon learned what it meant to "fall",
To buck the logs, to set the chokers and such.

He never told me that logging was rough.
He just said, "You look big enough,
And I'm going to make a logger out of you."
I was about fourteen, I guess,
When I found myself in the wilderness,
Where I learned to do things that a logger had to do.

It wasn't long till I found out that,
The trees don't grow where the ground lies flat.
In fact, some were standing on end!
Now I thought that this was one hell of a place,
Because the hills were as steep as a billy goat's face,
And those loggers had to be a special breed of men.

Well, I learned to log, and I learned to fight.
I also learned to keep my mouth shut tight.
Because from a green-horn kid, they didn't want a lot of lip.
We lived four men to an old bunk house.
The bug you saw, no doubt was a louse,
And when our clothes got wet, we hung them up to drip.

Continued…

I soon learned how to get along.
I "wised" right up, and I got strong.
I also learned how a logger spends his pay,
He'd go to town on a Saturday night.
If he didn't get drunk, he'd have a fight,
And be sick as a dog the following day.

I decided then that this wasn't for me,
Because getting so drunk I couldn't see,
Soon made me change my ways.
It took twenty-five years of being a fool,
Before I quit logging to work for the school,
And you can bet I've never regretted a single day.

Now, it's been almost twenty years,
Since I quit the woods with the danger and fears,
And I'd like you to know that everything is fine.
I still recall the days and the times that we had,
When I worked in the woods, with my old dad.
As memories return to haunt my mind.

But I wouldn't go back to those "good old days",
That memory brings back in a sort of haze.
In spite of all those thrills.
The days we spent were hard and rough.
The job we did was dangerous and tough,
And besides, at sixty-five, I'm over the hill.

April 1971

THE BOWLING OF DAISY MAGOO

A bunch of the guys, were whooping it up,
Down at the Woodburn Bowl.
You couldn't have found a sober one,
In the house, to save your soul.

When out of the night, that was black as coal,
And into the din of the place,
Slipped a lovely young thing, already to swing,
With a silly grin on her face.

She was the kind of a woman that held your gaze,
With a sort of hypnotic stare.
In a skin-tight shirt and mini-skirt,
She was enough to make a man swear.

She was well endowed, standing straight and proud,
About the sexiest dish I'd ever seen,
She had what it took, to make a man look,
The second time, if you know what I mean!

Her eyes were as bright as a moon-lit night.
The most beautiful shade of blue.
Her face was the face of an angel,
And the rest was OK too.

Continued...

Continued...The Bowling Of Daisy Magoo

She stood and gazed, like a soul half-crazed.
She covered the room at a glance.
She scanned the face of each man in the place.
Then stopped, as if in a trance!

I tried to figure just who she was,
In that mini-skirt of red.
But the fellow that seemed to watch her the most,
Was the joker we called Ted.

Quickly, she walked across the floor,
And approached lane number four.
She cuddled that ball like a tender child,
As we wondered how she would score.

It didn't look like she had what it took,
To even lift the ball.
Nor did she care that she was watched,
By everyone in the hall.

Firmly now, she grips the ball,
And on the line she stands.
All eyes are turned upon her,
As she calmly dried her hands.

Continued...

But then the rack was ready.
She rolled her ball, at last.
She scored a perfect pocket hit,
In fact, it was a blast!

Eleven times she rolled that ball.
Eleven times she got a strike!
Eleven times the rafters rang.
We'd never seen the like.

And then she turned and faced;
Concentrated on her spot.
Once more she laid that ball out,
And it traveled like a shot!

I moved my head so I could see,
The pocket, when it hit.
She left the seven-ten pin split.
We heard her holler, "Shit!"

The women screamed. I heard a shout.
All eyes were turned her way.
She stood with hands upon her hips,
Unbelieving, and in dismay.

Now I'm not as dumb as some of these bums.
It happened just like I said.
The guy that kissed her, and pinched her ass,
Was that no good fellow, called Ted!

February 1978

THE OLD LADY WHO LIVED IN A SHOE
(A Modern Version)

There was an old lady, who lived in a shoe.
She had so many children; she knew not what to do.
Why, no one would blame her for flipping her lid,
For doing the things, they said that she did.

Tell me, my friend, just what would you do,
If shoe laces were found, in your mulligan stew?
And all of those children had no place to play.
How would you feel, and what would you say?

Can you imagine the hub-hub and noise,
That could come from that many girls and boys?
Imagine fixing lunches for that many kids,
And all of the mischief, that most of them did?

How about buying shoes for that many feet.
And keeping seat-covers on each little "seat".
The time it would take to wash each little face,
And to keep things picked up and put in its place.

Just one more question, I would ask, please,
What ever happened to the father of these?
We all know that this woman lived in a shoe.
Can we not assume that a man lived there too!

We can also assume that he must have been tired,
And lame in the back, from all the children he sired.
My theory is this that he gazed at his brood.
He decided that this many kids, was not good!

He stood there in wonder, disbelief, and dismay!
Then slowly shaking his head, he wandered away.
Now I'm told, the old lady, showing no grief,
Went right to the County and got on relief.

June 1977

111

ME AND THE HUSTLER

Now I used to think I was pretty good,
With a pitching wedge, or a number two wood.
And I wasn't above hustling a five or ten.
Well, the more I played, the better I got,
Until I thought I was pretty hot.
And all a fellow had to do, was just say when.

I was practicing my putting, on the putting green,
When this fellow came up, who I'd never seen,
And asked me would I like to have a game.
My eyes lit up with a dollar sign,
And a little tingle went up my spine,
And I said, "Sure, but you'll have to keep it tame."

He asked me what I thought about three.
I answered that, that would be fine with me,
I'd have to get my clubs, and meet him on number one.
When he walked up with that bag of clubs,
I knew for sure that he wasn't a dub.
In fact, I wasn't sure that this would be any fun.

He said for me to lead the way,
As he hadn't yet been on the course to play.
I took a five from out my bag and laid it up.
He took his wedge and a practice swing.
He teed up his ball and when he hit the thing,
It went out of sight, but landed by the cup.

Continued...

Continued... *Me And The Hustler*

Where my ball came to rest, there wasn't any grass.
In fact, it was bare as a billy goat's ass.
And before I knew it, I was laying three!
He tapped his in for a birdie two.
He says to me, "How many for you?"
I said, "I guess, I'll have to take a bogey four."

He used a number one wood from the number two tee.
That ball went further than I could see.
In fact, I never saw that ball come down!
I hit my ball about two-twenty-four.
Then I hit it about two-twenty more,
And finally got up to where his ball was on the ground.

Well, this went on from tee to tee.
I'd get a four and he'd get a three.
And really it's enough to make a man feel sick.
From the first to the ninth, he never let up.
He just kept dropping them in the cup,
And I was beginning to feel like a hick.

I learned that no matter how good you are,
There is always somebody that's better by far.
And that it hurts to learn the awful truth.
I lost twenty-seven bucks on the first nine holes.
I couldn't do a thing right to save my soul,
It's times like these, you become a man and lose your youth!

I never found out, the man's last name,
But I tell you he played one hell of a game.
And I learned from him a thing or two.
Never bet 'til you know how the other guy plays.
Believe only half of the things that they say,
For taking your money is the best thing that they do!

November, 1977

HOW EDITH WENT CLAMMING

We watched her grip the shovel
As across the beach she trod.
Her fear is neither man nor beast.
Her faith is in her God.

She said, "I will surround them.
I'll hit them where it hurts.
I'll walk right by the little squeaks,
To where the biggies squirt."

Now, out upon the sand bar,
Like a hound dog, on a scent,
With disregard for the rolling surf,
She proceeded with dead intent.

At last! With nerves a 'quiver,
She spies the sign she sought.
Her knuckles turned a deathly white!
Her muscles "bow-string" taut.

Like a rattle snake that's striking,
Her shovel strikes the sand!
Wildly now, she grovels,
And in haste, she cuts her hand.

Continued...

With her blood streaming on the beach,
And glistening in the sun,
She swears at everything in sight,
And then cuts the other one.

She cries, "Give up! You fiend, with fangs;
You beast, beneath the sand."
With wild and renewed vigor,
She wildly wields her brand.

With her shovel firmly planted,
She makes a mighty pass!
The handle snaps, and breaks in two,
And "Ede" lands on her ass!

With the tide about her swirling,
She sits flat upon the beach.
Her eyes are large as saucers.
Her shovel's out of reach.

Cap doubles up with laughter,
At the sight which he beholds.
His good wife on her "one spot",
In that ocean, icy cold.

Oh, how much I would have given,
To film this hilarity,
To give to future generations,
Of Edith's posterity.

May 1979

THE FRINGE
UPON THE BEDSPREAD

There are many things that bug a man,
As he goes through his life.
A girlfriend that might be pregnant,
Or a whining, nagging wife.

But the worst thing I can think of,
When all is done and said,
Is the fringe upon the bedspread,
That my wife puts on my bed.

On this bedspread there are tassels,
That can clutter up my sleep.
Should I find them in my nose, and mouth.
Sometimes I almost weep.

For when I'm weak and weary,
And my eyes in sleep would close,
I find the tassels from the bedspread,
Are dancing in my nose.

When at midnight's eerie striking,
I awake and find I've rolled,
And that bedspread, from my falling,
Leaves my "one-spot", blue with cold.

My brain is numb with slumber,
As if I've had too much to drink,
When I find them "dad-burned" tassels,
Playing leap-frog with my "dink".

Now, you know it is no wonder,
That I face each night with dread,
From the fringe upon that bedspread,
That my wife puts on my bed.

November 1977

THAT COLD-SHOULDER NO

Before you get married, your girlfriend so sweet,
Lays all that she has on the ground, at your feet.
But after the wedding you find out too late,
It still is all yours, but you'll just have to wait.

You court her, and kiss her, and give her presents.
You wine her, and dine her, until she consents.
Well, the wedding is over. You've had your last date.
She then gets a headache, and you'll just have to wait.

You go "Honey-Mooning", and you think things are fine.
You shower and you shave, because you know that it's time.
But she gets into bed, wearing all of her clothes.
I guess one would say, that's a cold-shouldered NO.

When Mother's Day comes, as it does once a year,
You get all excited, because your time is here.
You hug her and kiss her, as your love you would show.
She then turns you off, with a cold-shouldered NO.

Father's Day gets here, as it does every June,
And as the time approaches, you whistle a tune.
Your Father's Day present was paid for with your own dough,
And she takes the wind from your sails with a cold-shouldered
NO.

Thanksgiving's the time, to be thankful, you bet.
And you know that you're grateful, for the little you get.
You look forward to an evening, that must be just so,
But your hopes disappear with a cold-shouldered NO.

Now it is well known that some do and some don't,
But why must my wife be the woman who won't.
God knows that I love her from her head to her toes,
And I pay no attention to those cold-shouldered No's!

April 1975.

117

THE CURSE OF A SNORING WIFE

For fifty years, my wife and I,
Have shared a common bed.
For I am not the kind, to try and find,
Another one instead.

Yet, I am sorely tempted,
To leave my love's delight.
And find someplace to lay my head,
Where I might *sleep* at night.

For my wife is now a snorer.
My patience now has fled.
While she sleeps and snores the entire night,
I lie with aching head.

When she snores the curtains flap.
The shades roll up and down.
The neighbor's dog begins to bark,
And the hobos all leave town.

She will take a breath, and hold it.
I swear she has breathed her last!
She moans, and groans. She grinds her teeth.
Then exhales with a blast.

Continued...

Our tom cat heads for cover.
Our poodle wets the floor.
The pictures rattle on the wall,
As the blast, blows shut the door.

It is then, I gently nudge her.
"Turn over, Dear", I said.
"Your snoring's getting long and loud.
I fear you'll wake the dead".

Now, no jury would convict me,
If I were to shoot her dead.
Then take my clothes and flee the house,
To seek some another bed.

I'm sure I'd be acquitted,
For the torture that I've stood,
Since I agreed to marry her,
And share the life that's good.

So, for tonight, when we retire,
My silence I will keep,
When she retorts, "how can I snore?
I've not yet been to sleep."

November 1977

GETTING A PHYSICAL

I retired at sixty-four.
Tired, but happy, and what's more,
I vowed that I would live a life of ease.
So I decided, first of all,
That I would pay the "doc" a call,
Just to be sure, that I was free from all disease.

Well, I combed my hair, and washed my face,
And headed for that doctor's place,
Where the cutest little nurse, made me disrobe!
And to get upon a table, where this nurse,
(Who's name was Mabel)
Began to poke me here, and there, and pry, and probe.

Now the 'nightie' that she gave me
Was not long enough to save me,
Because it didn't hardly cover anything, almost!
I could hear them nurses chuckle,
(At my knees that looked like knuckles)
And I know my body's not the kind, of which I'd boast.

Well, this cutie, says to me,
"Come on, handsome, follow me.
I am going to take you to the X-Ray room."
Now, when she called me handsome,
I almost flipped my transom,
And was glad she could not see me, in full bloom.

When she asked me, was I able
to lie down upon the table,
I figured just for her, that I'd make do.
But when my "hiney" hit that metal,
It was awfully hard to settle,
Because I knew that my "back-end" was turning blue.

Continued...

She finally gets the X-Ray, as my mind
Goes 'round and 'round.
I would really like to know what's going on.
She takes the pressure of my blood
And pronounces that it's good,
Then continues down the hallway on the run.

I end up in a room, rather small,
And full of gloom,
With a lot of little bottles on a shelf, upon the wall.
From all the indication,
She wanted urination,
Into a wee bottle, with an opening, way too small.

I knew not what to say,
As she turned and walked away,
And before I tried to say it, she was gone, just as before.
So as I tried to concentrate,
Into the jar I'd urinate.
I found that I had only dribbled three small drops upon the floor.

Now as I stood there waiting,
For that nurse, with breath abating,
I could not help but wonder how a woman filled a jar?
For a female never came with,
What it really takes to aim with,
But without what she had, this old world could not go far!

It wasn't long until she came back
To the place, where I was waiting,
And I knew that things would start to happen pretty soon.
When she came back in the room
With a needle in her hand,
I knew that very shortly, I would sing a different tune.

Continued...

Continued... *Getting A Physical*

Now, I figured, by the by,
I was scoring pretty high,
And when I looked around, she reappeared.
She says, "I need some blood",
Which to me, don't sound so good.
But as no one else was in the room, I volunteered.

It was then I heard her say,
As she turned and walked away,
Would I please follow as she walked down the hall?
I could tell by all the moans,
All the shrieks, and cries and groans,
That I was about to see the doctor, after all.

Then, he told me about his ex-wife,
Asked about my golf, and sex life,
And a dozen other things as he calmly paced the floor.
He then laid me on a couch,
Made me wince, and holler "ouch"
As he poked his finger into places, where no man had poked
before.

Well, he punched, and pushed, and pried,
And it seemed to me,
He tried just to see if he could find out how many tender spots I
had.
But the worst of all was when,
To examine my rear end,
He used a plumber's helper, which truly made me sad.

He tells me to come back,
In a year, or two, or three,
And we'll do the same thing over, just to keep me up to "snuff".
But I don't think I ever will,
For when I received his bill,
I decided then and there, that once within my lifetime was enough!

1974

A MEDLEY OF LIFE AND TIMES

When my doctor one day told me,
I had cancer on my "thing",
I guess, you know, right then and there,
My life plumb lost its zing.

Because me and that old "Buddy",
Had been down the road a spell.
With what I'd seen and all I'd done,
I would have a lot to tell.

Long ago I met a lady,
Who turned out to be my wife.
The kind you sometimes read about,
Who made for me a life.

We had a home with happiness!
A house, plumb full of love!
The kind that poets write about,
That comes down from above!

Children? Yes, we had them.
There was two of each, I guess,
There would have been a whole lot more,
If Mama would have said, "Yes".

When you have three strikes against you,
When the umpire says, "You're out!"
There's no use to start in swearing,
Or to throw your weight about.

Next time you must try harder!
Not to get blinded by the sun.
Just swing a little truer,
When you've got 'em on the run.

Date Unknown

THE SIN OF FOOD

Please give me strength, to just say "NO",
When, I find, I'm where the salads grow.

Where whipped cream, piled so high and yummy,
Wrecks its havoc with my tummy.

Olives, green or black, I love 'em,
And cornbread, fresh from out the oven.

How I drool at crispy chicken,
Southern fried, and finger lickin',

With mashed potatoes, fluffed and wavy,
Hiding 'neath that luscious gravy.

And 'though I see these pounds of grease,
Piling up, I just cannot cease.

But how I love those breakfast rolls,
And donuts, with coconut, and holes.

And for the present, I'll not quibble.
I'll just let that syrup dribble.

I'll let the pounds land where they may,
And I won't care what people say.

The fact I'm fat, I'll not admit,
Although my Levies fail to fit,

And this blob of fat that is my waist,
Put there, my friend, by mayonnaise.

Which is a fact, I'm no denying,
I'll be eating pie the day I'm dying.

February 1974

DISGUSTING, AIN'T IT?

It seems that man is just a slave,
To pomp and circumstance.
His number's up right from the start.
He doesn't have a chance.

You get a cane and comfort shoes.
You wear a hearing aide.
Your relatives start waiting,
For all the dough you've made.

You try to get back in the pink.
You do the best you can,
By using natures remedy,
And taking "Seratan".

You wear a dressing gown to bed,
Wool socks and underwear.
Your bustle starts to sagging,'
And your frame shows wear and tear.

You get up in the morning.
You do your exercise.
You worry about your figure,
And get bags beneath your eyes.

Well, you end up wearing glasses,
And you wear a wig or two.
You spend your time wondering,
Just what the neighbors do.

Now when these little items,
Are added one by one,
To each of us, we will admit,
It's been a lot of fun!

Date Unknown

HALLOWEEN

It's Halloween, the black cats cry.
Goblins howl and witches fly,
And on a limb in a cedar tree,
An old owl sits just as plain can be.

Now and then you'll hear him hoot,
When he does, the goblins scoot.
But spirits take their time to stroll,
Because he is a kindred soul.

It's now that pumpkin heads appear,
With hollow eyes and faces queer.
With eyes made live by candle light,
That gleam and flicker in the night.

While on some dark and eerie street,
While walking on, you'll surely meet,
Goblins scooting here and there,
Wearing masks with stringy hair.

The little ones, come to us for treats,
From house to house, on down the street.
Each one watches, bright of eye,
Hoping no spirits he will spy.

All kinds and sizes of clowns and hags.
All dolled up, and all with bags.
Now should you listen as monsters you meet,
You'll hear them cry out, "Trick or treat!"

We soon lose count as by the score,
They come and knock upon our door.
Though we sometimes think it weird,
We'll wait for Halloween next year.

October 1970

I'M THANKFUL
THANKSGIVING IS OVER

It has been seven days since Thanksgiving.
I recall all that fattening food.
Four times I went back to fill up my plate,
Because everything tasted so good!

So now, it is one week later.
The food that I see, leaves me cold.
I am sure you'll agree, there's no romance,
In a turkey that's seven days old.

For days we have eaten cold turkey.
The dressing is dried out, and stale.
I find that which is left, for my dinner,
Is a very small piece of his tail.

The salads, once garnished and gaudy,
Have all disappeared down the drain.
What hasn't been put in the garbage,
I have on my plate, once again!

Now as I sit here, Lord, of all I survey,
May I please make a note in the log.
I am thankful, Dear Lord, for all that I have,
But could I please, just have a "hot dog".

December 1970

WELL, IT'S ALMOST TIME FOR SANTA CLAUS

Well, it's almost time for Santa Claus, to come again this year,
To bring to us, all those pretty gifts, and all that Christmas cheer.

It's said he's spent the entire year, making all those wondrous things.
All those toys, for girls and boys; the dolls, and guns, and golden rings.

Yet, it seems there's something phony! And a whole lot could be said,
About a gent, whose time is spent, running 'round, dressed up in red!

Whose only transportation, is some reindeer and a sled.
Who never comes to visit, until everyone's in bed.

Then there is still, this other thing, which we all know is true.
Why can't he enter at the door? Must he come down the flue?

To scatter ashes on the rugs, and soot, about the room,
As he snoops about the premises, and roams around the room.

I've watched this guy, for many years, I'm onto every trick.
The way he flies about the skies, he really is quite slick.

Then there's this thing, about that sled, he uses every year.
The way it floats about the roofs, to me, is mighty queer.

There also is some question, as to the fuel that Santa needs,
To keep his sled a flying, and "deer power" in his steeds.

From tip to head, I've searched that sled, to find what makes it go
Through rain and wind, so effortlessly, and ice, and sleet, and snow.

Date Unknown

CHRISTMAS DINNER AT DOT'S

She had cleaned the whole house from bottom to top.
She had swept with the broom, and scrubbed with a mop.

She had set the table with the utmost care,
With her very best china, and bright silverware.

The Christmas décor was a joy to behold.
The candles, all burning, the angels of gold.

There was holly, and tinsel, and mistletoe too.
A fire brightly burning, sent smoke up the flue.

Oh! That turkey was really a beautiful bird.
Roasted and basted, down to the last word.

There was light bread and hot bread. There was jelly and jam.
There were fluffy potatoes, and southern cooked ham.

What with pickles, and relish, and cranberries too,
Olives and onions, to name just a few.

Then came desserts before my very eyes,
All kinds of goodies, from cookies to pies.

Her dinner was planned with the utmost of care.
She knew that her guests, soon would be there.

Continued…

Then out on the street, there arose a great din.
The smashing of fenders, the bending of tin!

Then what to my blood-shot eyes should appear,
But all of her kin folk, screaming for beer.

On to the doorway like locusts, they came,
Where Dot met and kissed them, and called each by name.

There was Alan, and Lynn, and Robin, and Sue.
There was Rick and Anne, to name just a few.

There were the Palmers, and Rick's pretty wife,
And Anne's husband, Ron, just bigger than life.

Michelle and Katie were dressed all in blue.
Grandma Scharborough had come over too.

There were drinks all around.
There was hugging, and kissing, and then with a bound,

Away to the table they tore like a flash,
As soon, what was left, looked like yesterday's hash.

Then, like the leaves that before the winds fly,
They all began leaving, and saying, "Good-bye".

Then I heard someone saying, "Oh, be of good cheer.
For we all will be back for dinner next year."

December 1973

HOW BLANCHIE WAITED FOR SANTA

T'was the night before Christmas; it comes once a year.
With plenty of presents, and lots of good cheer.
Now this is the way that it really should be,
But dear old Blanchie, was not drinking tea.

Nobody was coming. She knew none were near,
So she decided, that she'd have a beer.
While she waited for Santa to come down the flue,
She set out a couple; he'd want one or two.

And just to feel better, although it a sin.
She drank up some whiskey, and also some gin.
But in waiting, the time had somehow flown by
And Blanchie was starting to get pretty high.

When all of a sudden she heard a loud scream,
And Santa had landed, right smack on his beam.
His clothes were all old. His shoes kind of shoddy.
He wrinkled his nose, and sniffed for a toddy.

He drank all the beer. He sampled the gin.
He took a big drink, and wiped off his chin.
As he turned to his work, dear Blanchie, he spied.
He started to laugh. He laughed till he cried.

Blanchie then wondered just what he would do.
Well, he took one more drink, and climbed up the flue.
And she heard him call out, through the night, bright and clear,
"Merry Christmas to all, and thanks for the beer".

Now this all happened a long time ago,
'Cause Blanchie's sworn off booze, she don't drink no mo'.
Should you want a moral, you'll find, I believe,
That it pays to stay sober on each Christmas Eve.

Date Unknown

IT WAS THE
DAY AFTER CHRISTMAS

It was the day after Christmas, at my house.
I had stood about all I could stood.
My in-laws had gathered like locusts,
To drink, and eat up all my food.

For weeks I have watched Christmas shoppers,
As they push, and they shove in the stores.
Now all that is left is the shambles,
In the basement and three upper floors.

So, for a change I went to a party.
The Tom and Jerri's were built kind of stout.
The windows were trimmed up with tinsel,
And little angels were flying about.

A fire in the fireplace was burning.
The coals were glowing and red.
The hi-fi was playing "Joy to the World".
You could not hear a word that was said.

The kids were all fighting and screaming.
The dog was chasing the cat.
When some dirty old son-of-a-gun,
Put a marshmallow right where I sat.

Everybody was having a good time.
We all had a drink in our glass.
When the hostess tripped, on a rug on the floor,
And landed right flat, on her --- (face).

We helped her get up, and gave her a drink.
When she said in a voice, loud and clear,
"Happy New Year to all, and may that great speckled bird,
Flap his wings as he flies in your ear."

December 1970

SPECIAL THANKS TO:

William
Auntie
Grandpa
Mom & Dad
The Gabby Girls
Monte & Robin
The whole "Fam Damily"
My pals at work
My dear friend Mary

Howard Taft Palmer, although not an educated man, had a wonderful way with words which allowed him to express himself through poetry. His words reflect the beauty and love that he found in everyday life. He truly believed that nothing existed in this world except by the grace of God.

If he left us a legacy to be carried forth, it was his love of life and the belief that some good exists in everything.

He was like the covers of this book, with its rough edges, and the grain of wood that reflectes the strength and beauty that was the man.

Throughout our lives there were many times his heart ached from some thoughtless deed that one of us may have done. Yet, no matter what, there was never a time that his love and understanding did not show through and above his hurt and anger. He is gone from us now but the memory of his love and understanding will remain with all who knew and loved him.

It is therefore with fond re-membrances of this man who was our father, that we lovingly dedicate this book of his work.

Howard 'Monte' Palmer,
Bobbe Clair Gurley,
Bonnie Palmer,
Charles 'Robin' Palmer,
December, 1989

It was Christmas 1989 when I received the best gift ever, a collection of poems, 150 plus by Howard Palmer, my Grandpa. Bound together between crude pine wood covers were all the poems my mom, Bobbe Clair, could assemble each hand typed on plain white paper.

I always thought he was wonderful; he was my grandpa, for goodness sake. But imagine on the day of his memorial, the church was overflowing with those who loved and admired the man I still consider my hero.

Please enjoy Grandpa's work,
Bonnie Claire